More Memories

of

Manchester

Edited by Chris Makepeace

The publishers would like to thank the following companies for their
support in the production of this book

Main sponsor
Martins Bakeries Limited

Fred Aldous Limited

Brooke Bond

Capes Dunn & Company

A Carey & Son Limited

Cerestar UK Limited

Cobbetts

Henry Cooke

Dunlop GRG Holdings

The Legendary Joe Bloggs Clothing Company

T Liggett & Son Limited

Manchester Airport

The Manchester Grammar School

The Manchester Rubber Stamp Company Limited

Montell Polyolefins

Royce Peeling Green Chartered Accountants

Scottish Courage Brewing Limited

Joseph Spark & Son Limited

JD Williams & Company Limited

First published in Great Britain by True North Books Limited
England
HX5 9AE
Telephone: 01422 377977
© **True North Books Limited 2000**

ISBN 1 903204 03 8

Text, design and origination by True North Books Limited
Printed and bound by The Amadeus Press Limited

The Manchester story

Where archaeology ends, written records begin, and although many tribes must have occupied the dense forests of Lancashire, we don't learn a great deal about this human occupation until the arrival of the Romans - inveterate record keepers. In 79 AD the Roman general, Agricola, established a camp at Castlefield, where the River Medlock ran into the Irwell. After the establishment of the fort, a civilian settlement gradually developed outside the walls.

A Market Town

Growth is often associated with trade, and in 1301 Thomas de Gresley granted 'the great Charter of Manchester' by which it became a free market town. The Market Place, the area between present day St Mary's Gate and Cateaton Street, began to thrive. Nearby, the tiny Norman church formed the nucleus of what would become Manchester Cathedral.

Turbulent Days

Manchester's story was not always to be one of peaceful growth. Standing for Parliament against King Charles I, the town found itself besieged by an army of 4,000 men in 1642. Around a century later, Manchester found itself in the midst of another battle. Supporting the government again, Manchester found itself occupied by the rebel army and its residents forced to contribute to the Pretender's cause.

'King Cotton'

In that same 18th century, the changes were underway that would transform Manchester into a great industrial city. The woollen textile industry has been a part of the town's economy since the middle ages, the earliest evidence being from the 13th and early 14th centuries. The skills were to be developed that could instantly be put to use when 'King Cotton' - waiting in the wings - made his entry. A series of inventions, mainly by Lancashire men and starting with Kay's 'flying shuttle' in 1733, transformed the infant cotton industry over the next 50 years. Production was mechanised, powered first by water and later by steam, and factories began to replace the domestic system. The Industrial Revolution had well and truly begun.

The sale of cheap cotton goods made in Lancashire was the driving force behind Britain's industrial supremacy in the 19th century, and at the heart of this revolution was Manchester. With 105 spinning factories established there by 1825, Manchester was being described as 'Queen of the Cotton Cities' in 1849. Not only did the city have its own textiles industry, but it served as the focal point for imports of raw cotton and exports of finished goods through Liverpool for a belt of cotton towns around Manchester. Business transactions on a world-wide scale were conducted at the Exchange, becoming the famous Royal Exchange in 1851.

Continued overleaf

Whilst this is a picture of VJ Day, the long bread queue shows that in some ways nothing had changed on August 15th 1945 and rationing still had Manchester, along with the rest of the country, in its grip

Manchester Central Library: Local Studies Unit

However, cheaply made goods soon became expensive without an efficient transport system. The roads in the North West were described as 'infernal' by Arthur Young in 1770. The Duke of Bridgewater made a breakthrough when he began construction of a canal from his coal mines in Worsley to Manchester in the early 1760s. It was partially opened as far as Stretford in 1761 and finally reached Manchester in 1764, including that 'wonder of the world', the aqueduct over the Irwell at Barton. The Bridgewater Canal was completed as far as Runcorn, where it entered the River Mersey, in 1776. Cheap but slow, was transformed to both cheap and fast when the Manchester to Liverpool Railway was opened in 1830. The first passenger railway station in the world was built at Liverpool Road, Manchester.

Urban Problems

There was another side to the golden coin of prosperity. From a town with a population of about 17,000 in 1750, and containing fields in Piccadilly, central Manchester's population grew to something like 186,000 in 1800, and to 500,000 by the end of that century. Overcrowding created terrible, disease-ridden slums, two of the worst areas being off Deansgate and in the area between Fennel Street and Ducie Bridge. In 1844, The Manchester Police Act laid down that all new houses should have 'adequate sanitary facilities', ie an ashpit or privy of some sort and although some slum clearances began in the late 19th century, due to industry and commercial expansion, this did not begin in earnest until after the first world war.

From Prosperity to Decline

Manchester entered the 20th century in a confident mood - 'Cottonopolis' - a powerful city in a powerful country. The opening of the Manchester Ship Canal in 1894 had made the city Britain's fourth most important port. Civic and commercial pride had been expressed in the construction of fine buildings such as the new Town Hall and the extended Royal Exchange in the 1870s. Within the first decade of the new century, novel forms of transport began to appear on the city's streets - electric trams and motor cars. World War I was a turning point. The cost of fighting the war, the loss of overseas markets and the rise of stiff foreign competition sent Britain into

A busy view of Victoria Street which dates from 1946

economic decline, Manchester with it. 'King Cotton' was deposed, and although the Royal Exchange was extended again in 1921, membership fell from around 12,000 to 7,000 or so in the inter-war years. Luckily Manchester was not entirely reliant on cotton (for example the first Ford cars in Britain were made in the city), but the 'hungry 30s' were a reality for many Mancunians.

The Bombs Fall

World War II introduced Manchester to the horrors of bombing. As an industrial city this had been expected, but private houses, public buildings and hospitals suffered, along with the factories. By 1945, 559 Mancunians had been killed. The blackout and rationing added to the misery, but one thing had returned - work, and plenty of it in munitions and aircraft factories.

The Post-War Transformation

If the Luftwaffe somewhat changed the face of Manchester, post-war redevelopment took the process a good deal further. From the middle of the 1950s, rising prosperity and industrial diversification saw Manchester on the move again. The Royal Exchange closed in 1968,

but the Arndale Shopping Centre opened in the 1970s, symbolic of the city's move away from 'Cottonopolis' to a centre of retailing, financial services and modern 'clean' industries. Some of the worst features of the industrial past were tackled, with huge rehousing programmes and the removal of accumulated grime from public buildings. Manchester's architectural heritage was not destroyed by redevelopment and stone cleaning has revealed the qualities of old craftmanship standing alongside more modern styles. Innovative as ever, traffic problems have been tackled not just by the Mancunian Way, but also by the ground breaking MetroLink trams of the 1990s. The image of Manchester is now a world away from the 'muck and brass' of that cotton empire. Perhaps part of the city's genius is its ability to fashion a new empire from the remains of the old - the Royal Exchange became a theatre; Central Station became the G-Mex Exhibition Centre in 1986. The Nynex Arena, opened in 1995, offers an unrivalled sporting arena in the heart of the old industrial city. Manchester has emerged as a truly modern city served by an international airport, a centre for commerce, retailing, finance, education, culture and leisure.

Contents

Manchester Central Library: Local Studies Unit

Around the city centre

A pleasant day in 1936 finds people strolling, chatting or simply sitting in the sun and admiring the well-tended Piccadilly Gardens. Of course, being Piccadilly there has to be some form of public transport around, and this view from Portland Street captures a rather fine pre-war single decker bus in the foreground - a sight to gladden the heart of any bus enthusiast. In terms of the skyline, the modern view is not much different from the 1936 one. The Rylands building, with its roof beacon which was put there apparently as 'an aid to aviators', dominates the centre of the background. This building of massive proportions was constructed in the 1920s as a warehouse for the Rylands family of cotton manufacturers. Another building in Manchester associated with their name has a totally different appearance. This is the Rylands Library in Deansgate, regarded as a Victorian architectural gem in red sandstone, and erected by a Mrs Rylands in 1899 to commemorate her late husband, John Rylands. The Piccadilly building is now a branch of Debenham's. Shoppers in 1936 could find a Woolworth's at the corner of Piccadilly and Oldham Street, shown on the far right of the photograph. It had been built in 1926, replacing the Albion Hotel.

Above: The growing traffic problem in central Manchester in 1953 is well illustrated by the numbers of cars parked on Cannon Street. The cleared space to the right (most likely a bomb site) is offering some off-street parking - at a price. Cannon Street has undergone several transformations over the past three centuries. From a fairly quiet residential area in the 18th century, it had become the principal street for merchants by the 1820s. The Peel family, which would produce the famous Prime Minister of the 1840s, Sir Robert Peel, had warehouses there. Charles Dickens frequently visited Manchester, and the origin of the Cheeryble Brothers' warehouse in 'Nicholas Nickleby' was one owned by the Grant brothers in Cannon Street. Hitler did his best to knock the street about a bit, but for several years after World War II it remained a healthy commercial area. Older readers might remember such names as C & J Clark, Boot and Shoe Manufacturers, or Laidlaw & Thompson, Ironmongers. With Arndale appearing around it, and in some cases above it, the heart seems to have gone out of Cannon Street. It acts simply as a conduit for traffic which can no longer use Market Street, with only the lively fruit and veg stalls giving any reminder of what it once was.

Above right: It's a rather grey day in 1936, but the cobbles and tramlines around Piccadilly Gardens and the Esplanade are clear enough to the eye. Amidst the bustle it seems strange to think that around 250 years ago the Esplanade was known as the Daub Holes, a place where clay was extracted for the repair of houses. A natural infill of water into the holes began, and by the late 18th century it was decided to create an ornamental lake. Such quantities of rubbish accumulated in the lake, dumped there by the rapidly growing population, that it became a danger to health. Staff of the nearby Infirmary complained bitterly, and in 1853 the lake was filled in to create the Esplanade. Statues rapidly followed, and the one to Sir Robert Peel, that champion of the free trade that was so essential to the prosperity of Manchester, can be seen on the left. The Royal Infirmary, which moved here in 1755, stood roughly where the Gardens are to be found today. The building dominated Piccadilly, the clock on its dome providing a familiar landmark until the Infirmary's demolition in 1910. Whilst this was in process an accident and emergency room remained open at Parker Street. The new Infirmary on Oxford Road was open in 1908 and officially opened by Edward VII in July 1909, by which time it had been operational for seven or eight months.

Cross Street in 1951 presents a busy scene, and amidst the older vehicles is one which would have been the last word in up-to-date family saloons - the split screen Morris Minor. Created in 1829, Cross Street has always been known for business rather than shopping, although Boots' the Chemists once traded there, as did the well-known bookshop of Sherratt & Hughes. The offices of the Road Transport and General Insurance Company can be seen to the right, a good example of the financial, commercial and industrial concerns represented on Cross Street. The old 'Manchester Guardian', along with its partner the 'Evening News', also found their homes on this street until the Arndale Centre development. The association of Cross Street and business, however, is surely best exemplified by the breathtaking sweep of the Royal Exchange. Created as a transactions centre for the growing cotton industry, it had to be extended several times, and much of the present structure was created between 1866 and 1874. At its height the Exchange boasted almost 12,000 members. Integrity was always the watchword of the members, and part of the quotation from the Book of Proverbs which runs around the dome is, 'A good name is rather to be chosen than riches....'.

An unbelievable throng of people floods down the pavements of Market Street on a wet Manchester day in 1953, and as it is only ten past eleven in the morning, it could well be the madness of Saturday shopping. The well-known Burton sign is visible to the left, a tailoring chain which boasted at least one store in most towns and cities. As the name implies, Market Street has always had a bargain seeking connection and as early as the 13th century a Saturday market was being held on land between the present-day St Mary's Gate and Cateaton Street - the old Market Place.

What we now know as Market Street was the medieval Market Stead Lane - an important route to the weekly market. It soon became a place to shop in its own right, lined with half-timbered buildings and regarded as 'cheap and cheerful'. However, by 1820 the renamed Market Street, with only a width of five yards at its narrowest point, was regarded as the most congested street in Europe. It had to be constantly widened over the next 15 years. These 1953 shoppers knew a thing or two about congestion - all worthwhile if the 'cheap and cheerful' aspect was still there.

Manchester Central Library: Local Studies Unit

Manchester Central Library: Local Studies Unit

Above: Cobbles, trams and wonderful old cars provide an evocative picture of Oxford Street as it was in 1937. The railway bridge carrying the line between Oxford Road and London Road (later Piccadilly) Stations provides the division between Oxford Street and Oxford Road. This route into the city centre was first proposed in 1790 in order to provide a direct entry from the southern districts of Rusholme, Withington and Didsbury. These fine old trams had rattled and swayed around the streets of Manchester since 1901, and were to do so until 1949, when Tram 1007 made the final journey and closed that particular era. Of course the 1990s MetroLink system meant a 'return from the grave', although the modern vehicles don't quite have the character of the old trams. Oxford Street has always been renowned for its entertainments, and at this Whitworth Street corner the grand old Palace Theatre still stands. First opened in 1891, and rebuilt in 1913, it attracted such stars as Marie Lloyd and Charlie Chaplin. It continues the live theatre tradition today with high quality opera, ballet and musical companies.

Above right: The Alhambra Cinema on Ashton Old Road, Openshaw, as pictured around the 1940s, bore only the faintest resemblance to the Moorish palace in Granada, but then music halls and cinemas have always been about dreams and transports of the imagination. Names like the Alhambra, or the Rialto, hinted at a touch of the exotic and mysterious, an invitation to escape from dreary streets and

mundane lives into a world of romance, glamour and excitement. Not that people needed much persuasion around the 1940s, for in this pre-television age going to the cinema was a major leisure activity, and queuing was commonplace. The Alhambra at Openshaw was one of those cinemas which began its life as a theatre, opening in 1909 and featuring music hall turns. The first flickering films had been shown in Manchester by a Monsieur Trewey, in the Free Trade Hall in 1896. The medium was here to stay and the Alhambra, built to hold 2500 and unusual for its time in having a cantilevered balcony, was converted partly to showing films. From 1916, however, the theatre element disappeared and films prevailed. The Alhambra served Openshaw well, but it did not survive the competition of television and closed in 1960.

Right: The camera has captured a tranquil scene on what is clearly a sunny day outside the Kardomah Cafe on Market Street in 1939. In spite of the mass distribution of gas masks, and the frantic increase in aircraft production, it was difficult for most people to accept the proba-

Manchester Central Library: Local Studies Unit

bility of war. As far back as 1936 the Prime Minister of the day, Stanley Baldwin, had stated that, 'The bomber will always get through'. Therefore the consequences of modern total war meant masses of bombs falling on unprotected cities, resulting in huge casualties. Little wonder then that people tended to 'bury their heads in the sand' and believe it would never happen. Nevertheless no one slipping into the rather classy Kardomah Cafe for a quiet cup of tea could have failed to notice the heavily sandbagged lower part, or the fact that mountains of sandbags in Albert Square and Piccadilly were being piled up to create air raid shelters. As it happened, when the fears turned to terrible reality just before Christmas 1940, the Kardomah Cafe escaped unscathed, although the nearby Old Shambles and Market Place suffered terrible devastation. Next door to the Cafe, the half-timbered Old Wellington Inn, a building dating back to at least the 16th century, was also a survivor.

Bottom: This is a rather artistic shot of Albert Square, framed as it is by the arch of Carlton House, and showing a gentle covering of snow. The year was 1950, and a collection of solid looking 'period' cars seems to crowd in upon the statues and the monument - a far cry from the pleasant open space of today, with cars banished and the railings gone. The snow lightens the gloominess of a winter's day, a gloom accentuated by the bulk of the Northern Assurance Buildings rearing up in the background. Nevertheless a good hot drink could be enjoyed at the Joe Lyons' tea rooms situated close to the Cross Street corner. In the foreground, Gladstone raises his finger in perpetual remonstrance, and beyond him stands the statue of the public benefactor Oliver Heywood. Pride of place, however, must go to the monument to Albert, Prince Consort to Queen Victoria, whose spire reaches high into the winter sky. The offer of the statue was made in 1862 and the construction itself took many years. It was officially handed over to the city in 1867. Prince Albert had been a popular figure in Britain, and his death was much lamented. This very fine monument was erected as a tribute to his 'public and private virtues'.

Bottom: The freedom to roam Albert Square did not amount to much in 1958, for the pedestrianised area was a much truncated version of the modern one. Today it is possible to wander across the setts to get some perspective of the Albert Memorial or the statues of Gladstone, Heywood, Bright and Fraser. No such tranquillity for the sightseers of the 1950s. To amble round in a distracted fashion ran the risk of being knocked down by a marauding bus or at least inhaling petrol fumes. The top right of the picture is dominated by the Town Hall, and its rather grimy appearance in 1958 was the result of fumes of another type - those generated by almost a century of industrial pollution. The gleaming white of the newly built structure to the left stands in stark contrast, but the archi-tectural merits of this austere building are nil as compared to the neo-Gothic magnificence of the Town Hall, which later stone cleaning was to reveal in all its splendour. Designed by Alfred Waterhouse, and completed in 1877, this monument to civic pride was reckoned to be the finest Town Hall in Europe. Its lofty clock tower dominates Albert Square, and amongst the building's adornments are the recurring symbols of the bee (for industry) and the cotton flower (the basis of prosperity).

Right: There are some nice contrasts in building styles in this photograph across Princess Street and up Clarence Street, close to Albert Square and the Town Hall. The rather stately grandeur of the Northern Assurance Buildings just edges in from the left, all balconies and scroll work, so typical of a pre-first world war edifice. Grand in its own way, but somewhat austere, the white shape of the old Midland Bank building

dominates the background. Designed by Lutyens in 1929, the structure stands on King Street, and has more recently become the HSBC building. Whilst Greg's Buildings, on the corner of Booth Street, have remained much the same, the structure just to the left has taken on a very modern glass and stone appearance. And what of the steel framework being erected by Carlyle Construction in 1954? This was to become Pearl Assurance House - white, square and very mundane. There are certainly some signs of the times as the pedestrians make the long haul across the zebra crossing, although the van looks ancient even by 1954 standards. A boy aged around 13 wearing short trousers was a common enough sight in 1954, for this was before the age of 'teen' fashion and the media promoting every changing fad.

Manchester Central Library: Local Studies Unit

Manchester Central Library: Local Studies Unit

both John and Hayley Mills. Less well remembered is the fact that the soundtrack music was composed by one Paul McCartney. By 1972, the building was adapted into no less than five cinemas, but after the Cannon Group took over in 1985, Studios 1 to 5 were abruptly closed down in 1986. After some years of neglect, the building was converted to the Dancehouse Theatre.

Top: Market Street stretches away into the distance and, as always, the traffic moves busily in the vicinity of Piccadilly. This rather fine photograph was taken from the BBC studios in 1957. The statue of Sir Robert Peel had gazed stonily from the Esplanade for just over a century, whilst all around him an ever-changing story had unfolded of horse-drawn vehicles, electric trams, trolley buses and motor buses. The late 1950s, however, marked the infancy of an even greater change - the rise of mass car ownership and less reliance on public transport as increasing prosperity allowed more families to buy their own cars. Perhaps the great symbol of this was the Morris Minor, a few examples of which can be spotted down below. Shops, of course, are always subject to change, but Lewis's store has been one of the great survivors in keeping Peel company. Opening in 1877 at nos 110 and 112 Market Street, and expanding rapidly, by 1890 it was hailed as 'the greatest show place of Market Street'. The Lewis's sign is visible towards the left, and the store is still there. A little way to the right is Wiles'. This was an 'Aladdin's Cave' of a toyshop for the young, but alas it has not survived.

Above: The Regal on Oxford Road, photographed here in 1959, saw many changes in its lifetime. It was opened as a brand new picture house in 1930, as a response to the enormous boom in audiences that was anticipated at the advent of the 'talkies'. In fact the building housed two cinemas, back-to-back on the second floor, and hence they were given the name of the Regal Twins, each seating 800. They were the last word in modernity and comfort. Each one put on a different programme, and in the opening week, one of the Twins showed 'High Society Blues', starring Janet Gaynor and Charles Farrell - great attractions of the time. Star Cinemas bought the Twin Regals in 1960 and refurbished them. They were renamed Studio 1 and Studio 2 in 1962. A well remembered film showing at Studio 1 in October 1967 was 'The Family Way' starring

Manchester Central Library: Local Studies Unit

High days & holidays

Willie the Whale looks friendly enough, and the little boy at the front is probably not wanting to escape out of fear, but more from a desire to get to some of the other attractions on the Children's Amusement Park at Belle Vue. Nevertheless 'Willie' himself was very popular at the Children's Zoo, and the largest feature, measuring 32 feet in length and 8 feet in height. It was an imaginative idea to have a small aquarium tucked away inside his tummy. On this sunny day in 1955, the kids then might have run off (they always have to run!) to the Helter Skelter, the Baby Karts,

the Miniature Railway or a host of other attractions. More were to be added, including the Lilliputian village of Miniland in 1966. For the adults, of course, there were always experiences that fell more into the 'white knuckle' category. The pleasure gardens were in the hands of the Jennison family until 1925. It was James Jennison who, in 1908, introduced the Figure of Eight Toboggan, a predecessor to the Scenic Railway and the Bobs. The latter had a fearsome reputation for pure terror, but not to student Vance Tutton. In 1967 he claimed a world record by enduring 325 successive circuits of the Bobs!

Below: The days when young men in large numbers took up engineering apprenticeships sadly have past. The decline in Britain's manufacturing base has seen to that. Some readers probably remember the times when apprenticeships were carefully structured within strict rules relating to progression and pay. Wages were often pitifully low to begin with, and usually there was night school to attend, but at the end of around five years there was the prize of skilled craftsman status, and perhaps a good job for life. Apprentices often felt at first that they were little more than tea-making 'dogsbodies', but this was their accepted lot, so there must have been something more deep-rooted than that to have caused them to go on strike at Switch Gear and Cowans in 1960. A few are putting on a cheery smile for the camera, but clearly something was amiss. This firm of electrical engineers had been based at Trafford since 1926, and in 1960 it had plans to expand onto a new site in order to deal with increased sales, especially railway contracts. Whatever the apprentices' grievance worse was to come, for after a takeover by English Electric in 1967, 500 workers lost their jobs the following year as the Trafford and Altrincham factories were closed down.

Bottom: 'Listen to those dancing feet'. It may not be 42nd Street, but these dancers on Belle Vue's open air dancing platform are giving it a whirl and enjoying it. What a wonderful and rhythmic sound that wooden floor must have made as the dancers foxtrotted around. Perhaps it was the best way to keep warm, for judging by the leafless appearance of the trees in the background it was not summer, and this is supported by the evidence of the warm clothing on view. The fashions give the clue that this was a 1930s shot and a time when there were plenty of alternative attractions at Belle Vue. The glimpse of the boating lake to the rear may be a reminder to some Mancunians of the 'Little Britain' and the 'Little Eastern', the two pleasure boats that used to ply around the lake. Then again the memories might be of the spectacular fireworks displays in a dramatic setting that used to take place at Firework Lake *eg.* 'The Storming of Quebec' in 1954, with soundtrack and 250 actors. As for the wooden dance floor, it was destroyed by a bad fire in 1958, although it had been used more as a roller-skating rink after World War II.

Manchester Central Library: Local Studies Unit

Out and about in Manchester

As well as the opportunity to watch or participate in a wide range of sport, the scale and scope of Manchester's leisure activities is enormous. The city's theatre tradition, especially around Oxford Street, is owed partly to the 19th century music halls, set up to provide cheap entertainment for the working classes, such as the Apollo and the People's Concert Hall. Theatres aimed to capture a wide social spectrum, and household names in this respect were the Comedy Theatre (opened in 1875) and the Theatre Royal (opened on Peter Street in 1845). The Palace Theatre and the Opera House have survived to the present day, and form part of the rich choice for modern day theatre-goers, along with more recent creations such as the Library and Exchange Theatres. Manchester's early cinemas sometimes began as converted theatres when the new medium of film gained instant popularity in the early 20th century; others were purpose built to serve the great inter-war cinema boom from the advent of the 'talkies' around 1930. Cinemas have been forced to adapt to meet the fierce competition of television and video entertainment, but cinema-going still remains a popular leisure activity in Manchester.

Eating out is a pleasant accompaniment to a theatre or cinema trip, and restaurants abound in the city centre. Good pubs are not hard to find, but two of especial interest are the Old Wellington and Sinclair's Oyster Bar. Not only have they a rich history, but they have the distinction of having been physically moved in 1997 from the Old Shambles to the Cathedral area. Cultural activities in every form have grown along with the city. The Free Trade Hall, rebuilt after the 1940 'Blitz', has been traditionally associated with the famous Hallé and BBC Philharmonic Orchestras. A fine Art Gallery is to be found on Mosley Street. Both Chetham's Library and the Central Library house impressive collections, whilst the Rylands Library stands as a Victorian memorial to a Manchester industrialist. The Museum of Science and Industry is closely linked to the city's heritage. Leisure, of course, may simply mean a walk in the park, and the 'city fathers' of old were well aware of the importance of green spaces. Hence the creation of such public recreational areas as Queen's Park and Philip's Park. Belle Vue was once regarded as one of Manchester's great open air 'playgrounds', but as an amusement park it remains now only as a happy memory.

The bandsmen of the Grenadier Guards leading a file of men through Albert Square in a parade dating from 1964.

Manchester Central Library: Local Studies Unit

High summer in Burnage, June 1956 - and it's pouring down! What a shame that rain threatened to mar the Golden Jubilee celebrations of Burnage Garden Village, but perhaps it was only a shower. This little community began as a social experiment in the early years of the 20th century, when there was much concern about the degree of poverty that social surveys had exposed amongst the working classes. It was a matter of great alarm that in Manchester, 8,000 out of the 11,000 would-be volunteers for the Boer War had been turned away as unfit. Many middle-class reformers saw bad housing as a crucial factor,

and the Garden Village movement emerged. In 1906 Manchester Tenants Ltd purchased an 11 acre site at Burnage, and 136 houses were constructed, all for renting. Each house had electricity and a bathroom; avenues had grass verges, and in due course became tree-lined; allotments and a recreation ground were created at the rear. At the heart of the village were tennis courts and a bowling green. Burnage Garden Village became a model for others around Manchester, and those who have lived there have always taken intense pride over it. 'Everything within our own little Empire', was the motto of the Village Association in the 1930s.

Manchester Central Library: Local Studies Unit

Above: It's standing room only at Piccadilly Gardens in 1959 as both tiers of seats seem to be full. The state of the weather is unclear, for although one or two jackets have been removed, the general state of attire seems to indicate a warm day at the most. Even if it had been boiling, the discarding of a jacket or a cardigan would have been as far as most people would have gone, in public at least. These were more inhibited times, well before the advent of shorts, skimpy skirts and 'crop-tops' as familiar hot weather wear. Whatever the clothing, to sit in these pleasant gardens was a privilege which could not have been enjoyed in the very early years of the 20th century. The area was occupied by the Royal Infirmary between 1755 and 1908. The Esplanade to the rear was an ornamental lake until 1853. After the demolition of the Infirmary in 1910, huts were erected on the site as temporary accommodation for the Reference Library, which had been moved out of the former Town Hall, on the corner of King Street and Cross Street. It was not until 1934, and the building of the new Central Library in St Peter's Square, that the Reference Library was properly rehoused.

Right: It was a hot summer in 1955, in the days when there seemed to be a lot more difference between summer and winter than there is now. The deckchairs are out and basking in the sun seems to be the order of the day at Piccadilly Gardens. Perhaps if you closed your eyes (as one or two have done), ignored the sound of the buses, and allowed the scents of the flowers to linger in your nostrils, you really could believe that you were in some sort of idyllic rural retreat. We all have our roots in the soil if we go back far enough, and even a huge urbanised area like Manchester was once a collection of settlements, dependent on farming. Various well-known families held land in the Piccadilly area, including the Ducies and the Mosleys. Amidst the clamour of modern-day Piccadilly, it takes rather a leap of the imagination to envisage it as Lever's Row, as it was up to 1812. The name of this quiet residential area was derived from the Lever family of Alkrington, who had extensive lands in the neighbourhood. Whether our 1955 sunbathers were lost in a golden dream of rural England or not, it would only have been a short interlude before it was back to reality.

Memorable moments

*A*bove: *The concept of Play Streets in the Manchester suburbs was an interesting one. These two youngsters on Gay Street, Hulme, certainly seem to be enjoying themselves in a traffic-free environment, and the sign prohibiting vehicles would give them a full day to go at. The year was 1958, but the waving of the large Union Jack had probably less to do with a royal occasion than with sheer exuberance and energy. Such streets as this, however, were rapidly disappearing in clearance schemes. Between 1951 and 1967, 33,000 buildings were demolished, to be replaced by a variety of* council housing to suit different family sizes. The idea was to create new communities containing day nurseries, schools, a library, shops, car parks and green open spaces. Further planning had produced the Moss Side Centre by 1972, and a move away from the tower blocks of the early 1960s to deck access blocks. More recently, low rise estates have been favoured. The Play Streets of the 1950s disappeared, but this was not lamented by all. A letter in the press from a night worker in 1953, complained bitterly about 'toys' left in the streets for him to trip over. They included hammers, shovels, axes, iron bars and manhole covers!

Belle Vue, in its boom years straight after World War II, had the facilities to play host to any number of outdoor events. Various arenas were able to feature parades, tennis, horse-jumping, speedway, stock car racing and athletics. In 1955 the All England Schools Athletic Championships were held at Belle Vue, and the competitors are pictured parading past the Mayor and other dignitaries in what is probably the opening ceremony. It was a hot summer in 1955, and both the shadows and the dress of the spectators seem to suggest a sunny day, perhaps an ideal one for athletics. It must have been a proud occasion for all the competitors, regardless of whether they received any medals from the patriotically draped table. Some of these young athletes may have reached the peak of their achievements at these Schools Championships. Others may have gone on to even higher things. Certainly in later years there were to be athletes from the Manchester area who would become household names. Shirley Strong won a silver medal for the 100m hurdles at the Los Angeles Olympics in 1984. Diane Edwards (now Modal) and her Sale Harriers team-mate, Ann Williams, came first and second in the 800m final at the Commonwealth Games in Auckland, in 1990.

Manchester Central Library: Local Studies Unit

It is uncertain what this occasion was in 1964, but clearly it was an important one. The bandsmen of the Grenadier Guards, instantly recognisable in their distinctive busbies, are leading a file of men swinging into Albert Square. Although in civilian dress, these men are perfectly in step, and their posture suggests military experience. The relay system, the seating along the front of the Town Hall and the canopy covered dais at the main entrance, all suggest an event of some note. And what better setting could there be than the Town Hall and Albert Square for pomp and ceremony? The Town Hall itself, completed to a design by Alfred Waterhouse in 1877, has a magnificent exterior which this particular photograph scarcely does justice to. However, the interior alone is enough to provide a fine context for any great occasion, with the history of Manchester depicted everywhere. Albert Square in some ways is a tribute to men of importance in Manchester's history, as expressed in statues and monuments. The one featured in the picture is of Gladstone, who appears almost to be conducting the band. Gladstone's brand of economic liberalism was very much to the taste of Manchester's 19th century businessmen and entrepreneurs.

Do you remember when....?

The memorable events in the life of a city such as Manchester consist of occasions when its people share in a great national event, or when something takes place that is mainly of concern to its citizens. The heady days at the end of World War II will stand clear in some people's minds - 'VE' Day and 'VJ' Day in 1945 - the singing, the dancing, the street parties. Manchester shared in the rejoicing of the entire nation that the long nightmare was over. Then there was the excitement of the General Election of 1945, and the visit of Winston Churchill to Manchester. People still hailed him as the man who had inspired the nation in the dark days, but they preferred to trust the future to others. Nevertheless, the post-war austerity years were rather gloomy until a landmark event - the Coronation of Queen Elizabeth II in June 1953. Damp though that day was, nobody who experienced it will ever forget the feeling that this was the dawn of a new era - another 'Elizabethan Age'. For many, the abiding memory is of watching the Coronation on a flickering black and white television, often in a communal hall, whilst clutching a Coronation mug. TV was here to stay, but how many of those mugs are still around? Since then, the only events to have captured the public's imagination in quite the same way have been the Silver Jubilee in 1977 and the wedding of Prince Charles and Lady Diana in 1981. Manchester has enjoyed plenty of visits from royalty and statesmen, but some have had more significance than others. The official opening of the Arndale Centre in 1979, by Princess Anne, was more than just a sightseeing occasion. It marked a transformation in the heart of Manchester, a landmark in the progress of the city from its old industrial base to a modern retailing centre. The opening of G-Mex in 1986, and Nynex in 1995, have been signposts in the same direction - Manchester as an exhibition and leisure centre. A 'straw in the wind' was the closing of the Royal Exchange in 1968 and the emergence of the Exchange Theatre - from textiles to thespians. At Ringway, the new Terminal 2 of 1993 announced Manchester Airport's importance to international travel, just as Manchester United's historic treble in 1999 heralded the city's status in international football. Not all memorable events are happy ones, and the Arndale bomb of June 15th 1996 remains grimly unforgettable. However, just as happened after the wartime 'Blitz', Manchester dusted itself down and began to rebuild.

Manchester City clear their lines in a game at Maine Road in 1960

Manchester Central Library: Local Studies Unit

Audiences of 7,000 were regularly admitted to King's Hall to see the Christmas Circus

Action replay

King's Hall at Belle Vue was the venue for a wonderful variety of entertainments during its lifetime. It was converted in 1928 into the building which became so familiar to so many people, and this 1940 picture shows a wartime occasion there. Boxing and wrestling were popular attractions, and in the music world the Hall played host to a range of superstars, including the Rolling Stones and Shirley Bassey. However, King's Hall is best remembered for some of the regular events it was associated with, such as the annual brass band contest or the yearly crowning of the Railway Queen. The Christmas Circus, conducted under the expert eye of Blackpool ringmaster George Lockhart, was a huge favourite, an eagerly awaited treat for many children. Audiences of 7,000 were regularly packed in to see such novelties as pigmy elephants and cycling bears. In tune with the times, King's Hall claimed to have the largest bingo club in the country between 1961 and 1966. Sadly, the 1960s and 1970s saw a drastic fall in the popularity of Belle Vue in general. The Zoo was closed in 1977, and in 1981 most of the main site was sold to developers. The final event at King's Hall before its demolition was the Christmas Circus of 1981-2.

A *sporting life*

Manchester has been able to provide an arena for all the major sports, but the two with the most consistent popular appeal have been football and cricket. Around 1879 a team of enthusiasts began to kick a ball about on land next to some railway shunting yards, giving themselves the name of Newton Heath. At much the same time, similar enthusiasm led to the creation of an outfit at West Gorton, who called themselves St Mark's. Little would these pioneers have known that what would evolve from these kickabouts would be two of the most famous names in British football - Manchester United and Manchester City. The two clubs have had varying fortunes in recent years, with United establishing itself as a leading European Club side, and City tending to lead a 'yo-yo' existence between the leagues. There is no difference, however, in the degree of passion which both clubs inspire in their supporters, whether the 'Red Devils' are being urged on at Old Trafford or 'Blue Moon' is echoing around the stands at Maine Road. Similar enthusiasm can be heard at Old Trafford in support of Lancashire County Cricket Club, for cricket is no longer the rather sedate affair it used to be in the days of Washbrook and Edrich. This particularly applies to one-day games, at which Lancashire have become specialists. The team's frequent visits to Lords to compete in the finals of such trophies as the NatWest, or the Benson & Hedges, have become 'party time' for the Lancashire supporters, with fancy dress and plenty of liquid refreshment. Using a differently shaped ball, there was success for Salford Rugby League Club in 1938-9 when it lifted the Challenge Cup. Sale, a premier rugby union team, provided the captain of the British Lions in the 1970s in the formidable shape of Fran Cotton. For those who prefer wheels for their sporting thrills, the famous cyclist Reg Harris appeared regularly at Fallowfield Stadium, in his heyday. The Belle Vue Aces have provided the roar of speedway since 1928, winning the British League Championship for three successive seasons in the early 1970s, whilst Peter Collins won the World Championship in 1976. In more recent years, local athletes Shirley Strong, Diane Modal and Ann Williams have between them won medals in the Olympic and Commonwealth Games. The 'state of the art' Nynex Arena, opened in 1995, is home to Manchester Giants (basketball) and Manchester Storm (ice-hockey).

Maine Road amidst the surrounding housing in an aerial view dating from 1970

More Memories of **MANCHESTER**

Below centre: The packed stands at Maine Road were probably 'oohing' and 'aahing' as the camera captures this dramatic moment in a game between Manchester City and Arsenal in 1955. City are on the attack, and the ball appears to be a blur as it is about to whip past an apprehensive Arsenal defender. City had a good team at this time, and Manager Les McDowall steered them to two successive cup finals in the mid-1950s, lifting the FA Cup in 1956. This was the era of the innovative 'Revie Plan', with Don Revie playing as a deep-lying centre forward - Hungarian style. It is noticeable too that the City players are sporting the new style 'V' neck shirts , as opposed to the more traditional collars of the Arsenal team. The 6-3 thrashing handed out by the Hungarians to England, in 1953, had convinced many that progress lay in adopting a more streamlined Continental kit, including 'V' neck shirts and low-slung boots - never a very convincing theory. Nevertheless, City had some outstanding players in the 1950s, including Jimmy Meadows, Ken Barnes, Joe Hayes and Bobby Johnstone. The rules, however, allowed them to earn no more than £20 per week - a far cry from the thousands of pounds earned by comparable players today.

Bottom: It's the 'beautiful game' in full flow as Manchester City clear their lines in a game at Maine Road in 1960. The advertisements above the packed stand in many ways give a flavour of the time. 'Mahogany Flake Tobacco' has a rich ring about it, and it is likely that there would be more pipe-smokers in a 1960 soccer crowd than today. Similarly, the Isle of Man and other domestic resorts would still have been the automatic holiday choice for most working people rather than a jaunt to the Continent. And what about that wonderful echo from the past, the Pakamac? Perhaps the manufacturers of this piece of plastic roll-up rainwear were hoping that Manchester would live up to its reputation when they advertised their product so prominently! The game of football was much the same around 40 years ago, but watching it was a whole different experience. Those were the days when home and away supporters mingled freely on the terraces, and at half-time there were often 'crocodiles' of people heading towards the end that their team would be attacking in the second half. All this to the accompaniment of a brass band on the pitch, whilst four youngsters carted a sheet around for pennies to be hurled into.

Manchester Central Library: Local Studies Unit

Manchester Central Library: Local Studies Unit

Manchester Central Library: Local Studies Unit

Manchester Central Library: Local Studies Unit

*A*bove: *Old Trafford in September 1959 may not have been as grand as it is today, and the catering now is a little more sophisticated than that of the 'hot pie' variety offered at the United Cafe, but one thing would have been no different - the passion felt for the team by the supporters streaming towards the turnstiles. Perhaps the passion has never been greater than it was in the immediate wake of the 1958 Munich disaster, with the memories of a great team so cruelly wiped out fresh in the mind. However, what a different sight the supporters of 1959 presented. Jackets and trousers are almost universal - no club shirts and trainers in those days! Manchester United had come a long way by 1959 from its humble beginnings as Newton Heath FC around 1879. The club played at North Road, next to the shunting yards, before moving to Bank Street, Clayton. Newton Heath re-formed itself as Manchester United in 1902, and moved to Old Trafford in 1910. Plenty of honours were to be won, but for these pictured supporters perhaps the greatest times lay ahead - from the historic European Cup Final victory over Benfica in 1968 to that astonishing 1999 treble of the Premiership title, the FA Cup and the European Champions Cup.*

Maine Road, one of the most famous grounds in the country, stands like an oasis amidst the surrounding housing in this aerial view of 1970. In its earlier incarnations, under the names of St Mark's (West Gorton), Gorton AFC and Ardwick FC, Manchester City had a number of homes including Clemington Park, Reddish Lane and Hyde Road. Whilst at the latter ground the club adopted its present name, and paid £5500 for the site of an old brickworks at Moss Lane. The new stadium of Maine Road arose from the rubble in 1923, a venue not only good enough for an

ambitious club, but grand enough also for FA Cup Semi-Finals. Safety standards were not as strict in those days, and the ground saw some colossal atten-dances. When Stoke City visited the ground to play Manchester City in a cup game in 1934, the gate was a huge 84,569. Maine Road as pictured in 1970 was a ground that was graced by the exciting attacking skills of Lee, Bell and Summerbee. City had won the League Championship in 1968 and the FA Cup in 1969. In 1970 the club lifted the European Cup Winners Cup. The ground had £6,000,000 spent on it in the 1992 improvement scheme.

The international flavour of a Manchester bakery

In 1996 the British Sandwich Association awarded first place in its competition to find Britain's Best Baker and Sandwich Maker to a chain of twenty-six shops in the Manchester area. In the words of the judges, the Manchester-based business had 'demonstrated its commitment to developing a quality sandwich business. Indeed to judge by customer comments Martins has established an enviable reputation for the services it provides to its takeaway customers'.

Martins Craft Bakers and Sandwich Makers has of course been a familiar name to Mancunians over many decades, but just who was Martin, and how did his sandwiches come to be judged the finest in the Britain?

The original Martin was one Richard Martin not, as might be supposed, a Lancastrian and a native of Manchester but instead a very far travelled man. Richard Martin was born in 1894, the son of Swiss confectioner Reinhart Martin and his wife Maria, in St Gallen in Switzerland. Reinhart Martin had established his own specialist bread bakery in St Gallen in 1892 after emigrating there from Tannenkirch in Germany's Black Forest. The Swiss Family Martin had four sons, one of whom eventually came to England. After training as an apprentice confectioner at Konditorei Weyer in St Gallen between 1911 and 1914 Richard appears to have been overcome with youthful wanderlust, working first in France then Ayr in Scotland and in Liverpool before finally settling down to work in Manchester at Sisson's bakers in St Ann's Square. Richard's brother Karl who had trained as a baker took over the Swiss family business in the 1920s and continued with the bakery and shop until the 1960s when it was sold to the Enderlie family, one of whom, Kurt Enderlie, had worked for Martin's in Manchester before continuing his career in Switzerland.

When Richard Martin opened his own Swiss Confectionery Bakery on the Tuesday following his marriage to Nellie Brayzier on Easter Sunday 1922 it was no doubt a revelation to the people of Moston. The Martins' first shop was situated next to the Ben Brierley public house, the terminus of the tramway and the stopping off place for people visiting Boggart Hole Clough with its boating lake and other attractions. Richard Martin's extensive range of continental confectionery, many made using his own father's recipes, soon attracted attention. The business began to flourish as a discerning clientele flocked to buy. Prices however were very different in those far off days - the first day's takings, a figure etched forever in Nellie Martin's memory came to one pound four shillings and three pence halfpenny. Just £1.23 in today's inflated decimal money, but then a fair day's takings given that in

Top: Richard and Nellie Martin in 1951.
Above centre: Richard's certificate which he received at the end of his apprenticeship.

WORSLEY AVENUE

MARTIN'S   CAFÉ

those days individual buns and cakes generally sold for just one penny each, or even less - and in those days remember we still had two hundred and forty glorious pennies in every pound.

At Moston the newly-wed Martins lived 'above the shop' Richard baking at the rear of the premises and Nellie selling from the front. There was almost

Above: *The Worsley Avenue shop to which Richard and Nellie moved in 1926.*

no mechanisation in those long gone times: Richard Martin relied on nothing more than his own expertise, muscle power , a Portway oven and quality raw material to establish his growing reputation.

And that was a reputation set to survive the decades. Some of Richard Martin's original recipes brought from Switzerland all those years ago are still being used today in Martins' justifiably famed range of continental confectionery.

With increasing sales an original loan from Richard's father in Switzerland was soon repaid. In 1926 with two new babies in the family, and just four years after starting their business, Richard and Nellie Martin moved to a new shop at 2 Worsley Avenue and built a new bakery at 32 Ivy Street, Moston where the business was to remain until 1994.

Business may have been generally good but life was difficult too. Shops remained open until 6pm daily and 9pm on Saturdays.

Paid holidays were not then the norm but with low National Insurance contributions and Income Tax at only 1/6 (7.5p) in the pound at least most of what the young couple earned stayed in their pockets.

With two separate premises to look after the increasingly prosperous business soon needed to acquire a van to move products between the two locations. The van was not however used for customer deliveries although doorstep delivery was very much the order of the day during the economically depressed times of the 1920s and early 1930s. Delivery of personal orders was by tricycle with a box on the front and racked out to carry

wooden trays. The younger family members were soon being roped in to help with deliveries, sometimes, if they were lucky, being rewarded with a whole penny!

If the 1930s were good for the Martins they were bad times for most, including Nellie's parents the Brayziers. Falling on hard times they were rescued by the Martins and ran a second shop for them at 1192 Oldham Road, a shop which could rely on a steady trade from passing mill workers still 'clogging it' to the mills in large numbers despite the economic depression.

The rise of Nazi Germany and the eventual declaration of war in 1939 inevitably led to changes for everyone in Britain and not least the Martin family and their business. Wartime shortages led to the introduction of bread and yeast goods to the firm when chocolate rationing made the production of quality confectionery almost impossible. In spite of the trying shortages, bombings and blackouts every effort was made to maintain quality. During the war years the introduction of sensible opening hours and the fact that what was made in the bakery always found a ready market with

Above: *The original bakery in St Gallen, Switzerland.*

absolutely nothing leftover unexpectedly proved to be a very efficient trading period.

After the second world war had come to its long awaited end the Martins opened a cafe at Worsley Avenue. Many people who were married at the local churches had their wedding receptions at Martins and, on a more sombre note, hundreds of people had their post funeral meal there with their loved ones 'buried with ham' as the local saying goes. Many a new husband will have memories of nervously delivering his speech to the assembled wedding guests at a Martins reception. Did you once make such a speech at Martins Cafe, or were you ever a bride or guest on such a happy occasion?

In 1952 Richard Martin was joined by his younger son, also called Richard. Richard Martin junior had previously served in the Merchant Marine for ten years. After young Richard joined the firm a thriving local bread trade was built up, capitalising on the additional expertise acquired during the war. That extensive bread trade is now a smaller but important part of the business today. Perhaps more importantly the ending of food rationing and the availability of fresh cream saw the welcome reintroduction of all of Martins' famed pre-war confectionery which found a ready demand amongst the sugar-starved, luxury hungry public. By the time Richard Martin senior retired in 1957 aged 63, after 35 years in the business, things were looking good. Richard Martin junior and his wife Pat enthusiastically embraced the family tradition, working hard for

Above: Early recipes for 'Penny Cakes' which formed the foundation of Richard Martin's business.

the future prosperity of Martins - and hoping no doubt that their young sons Neil and Ian might one day join the family firm too.

A third shop was bought in 1958, for just £1,750, from Armisteads in Moston Lane opposite Upper Conran Street. The bakery at the rear of that shop had a very efficient side flue oven ideal for bread baking to which the firm's bread production was soon transferred giving more room for confectionery production at Ivy Street and allowing output to increase by 50 percent.

It was in the 1960s however that the future pattern of Martins' growth became apparent with a still modest but steady increase in business. In 1962 an extension was made to the Ivy Street bakery and in the same year a shop at Failsworth was added to the growing chain - and the following year another at Chadderton. The Failsworth shop was a turning point for the business with the first week's takings there easily topping those of the parent shop in Moston.

In 1965 Harold Frances' fine bakery business opposite All Saints Church in Newton Heath was purchased bringing with it what were then phenomenal local bread sales. Times were good; deep freezing and other improvements to food technology helped ease production difficulties, but in a period of almost full employment and frequent strikes for better conditions and wages it was not easy to hold on to skilled workers.

In 1971 forty years of Martins history disappeared when their Oldham Road shop was demolished for a road widening scheme. A shop in Droylsden was bought to replace it.

Neil Martin joined the family firm in 1976 following a brief career in the Royal Navy; after working in the bakery for six months he concentrated on developing sales - particularly of sandwiches made in each shop. Neil's brother Ian joined Martins in 1978 after first spending two years in the merchant navy followed by a year working in a bakery in Southampton and four months honing his skills in the family's original bakery in St Gallen, Switzerland. Ian concentrated on production, introducing new lines and keeping pace with changing tastes.

The arrival of Ian Martin coincided with another watershed in the firm's history when the original shop in Worsley Avenue in Moston closed and the business moved to the former Burney's shop in the centre of Moston Lane. As a sign of changing times there were now just four bakery shops on the Lane - but there had been eleven just twenty years earlier.

In 1978 a new Martins shop was opened in Alkrington and sales were so good that the Droylsden shop was shut to allow the Martins bakery to cope with the increase in demand. The following year a separate cake bakery was opened in Ashley Lane, Moston to relieve pressure on the Ivy Street bakery which would itself later be

doubled in size to meet the challenge posed by ever increasing demand.

Martins Bakery loves nothing more than a challenge, and few things can be more challenging than baking a fifteen tier high wedding cake.

Above: Manchester Master Bakers annual dinner dance in 1951. **Right:** *The renowned 7ft 6ins cake of 15 tiers.*

In 1985 when Harpurhey man Joseph Doyle wanted to make his daughter Winifred's wedding day extra special he trod a path directly to the Martins' door. Was a fifteen tier cake possible? Of course it was, although at 7ft 6in tall the practicalities would not be easy, not even for a firm as renowned as Martins.

Construction however proceeded without a hitch; eventually costing £600, the fabulous Doyle cake weighed nearly three hundredweight and used 300 eggs, seven pounds of ground almonds and a whole bottle of rum. Martins have long been conscious of their social responsibilities as well as simply running a business which can respond to unusual orders for personalised confectionery. Many readers will recall the fund-raising appeal for Booth Hall Children's Hospital's intensive care unit in 1986. To help the £500,000 appeal Neil Martin famously produced the Bobby Bear Gingerbread biscuit featuring Bobby Bear with his arm in a sling. Bobby Bear was the hospital's mascot but it was

> *The firm moved from Moston in 1992 to occupy a former textile mill in Newton Heath*

Neil Martin who suggested the gingerbread version which sold in Martins for six years, during which time the company raised £20,000 for the Hospital's appeal fund.

Those who have watched the Martins' business grow will have recognised the 1980s as the decade in which it made the transition from being a medium sized firm to a large one. In those ten years Martins' grew from a chain of a mere six shops to one of nineteen, the critical point arriving in 1987 when Martins bought Laines bakers with its seven shops and a modern bakery in Salford near Boddingtons' Brewery. Martin's was becoming a major presence in Manchester - the 1982 opening of its shop in Cheetham Hill was even presided over by TV's Stuart Hall. The business was changing and reflecting that change, in 1987, after 35 years, Richard Martin retired from full time work and his sons Neil and Ian became joint Managing Directors.

Below: The Ivy Street Bakery.

In 1989 Martins bought the Lowes family business in south Manchester with five shops in Stockport, Edgeley, Levenshulme, Longsight and Chorlton. Since then, in addition to its own traditional repertoire of fabulous, mouth-watering confectionery, Martins has also been making Lowes' renowned lemon buns - try them once and Martins claim you will be hooked for life!

Production at the savoury bakery in Salford and the cake bakery in Ashley Lane Moston were transferred in June 1992 to International House a three storey Victorian former textile Mill in Newton Heath where the firm now has its headquarters. In January 1994 the last baking took pace at the firm's Ivy Street bakery and bread production was transferred to the modern 50,000 sq ft bakery built behind International House.

The firm now has a separate chocolate department making hand made chocolates. Martins prides itself on using only the finest Belgian chocolate; anyone who has tried one of Martins' justifiably famous Florentines is guaranteed to come back for more!

The Martins bakery makes produce only for its own shops - and makes everything those shops sell including cooked meats and all bakery and confectionery items. And yes, it is still possible to ask for cakes made to order. Customers wanting a special cake can choose from the photograph album available in each shop showing designs of a large selection of birthday, novelty and wedding cakes.

Alternatively customers can visit the firm's show room at its central bakery where most of its designs are on display and where customers can discuss their individual requirements with one of Martins' expert cake decorators.

Martins in Australia
In 1991 Ian Martin, his wife Val and their two young children, Kelli and Craig, emigrated to Australia maintaining the family tradition for travel; they have also continued the family tradition of baking.

Above: *Packing the freshly cooked bread.*
Top: *The textile mill at Newton Heath - the new home of Martins' Bakery since 1994.*

Since arriving Down Under Ian and Val Martin have opened a chain of Martins bakeries and coffee shops on Brisbane's Sunshine Coast with branches now in exotic sounding Buderim, Nambour, Maroochydore, Mooloolaba and Caboolture all in faraway Queensland. And even more are planned as the Martins name is franchised across Australia over the next few years.

The decade of the 1990s saw no slowing in Martins' growth, seven more shops being added to the chain during those ten years: Openshaw, Swinton, Heaton Moor and Withington plus six more when Sharples bakery shops were bought from the receivers in 1994.

The firm expanded in a different direction in 1998 when Martins Foods in Radcliffe was established following the purchase of C & D Patisserie to produce frozen hand-finished cakes and bakery products for supermarkets and coffee shops across the UK.

Each Martins branch is run by helpful friendly staff with high standards of hygiene and cleanliness and the best freshly baked food in the area. So proud are Martins of their facilities and their products and so confident of their standards that the public are even given an open invitation from Neil Martin to inspect the company's bakery.

Martins' 80 skilled bakers workers start making bread from 9.30 pm every night so that bread is fresh in the shop from 8 am.

There is perhaps nothing more evocative of the past than the smell of newly baked bread. And 'bread like it used to be' is one of Martins' catch phrases! The firm makes more than 30 varieties of bread 16 of which can be used to make a Martins sandwich. Hungry customers can decide which variety of bread, filling, salad and dressing to have in their sandwich in over a million combinations.

With a total staff of over 300 Martins now supplies 27 shops in the Greater Manchester area. How does the firm account for its ever-increasing prominence? According to Neil Martin 'We look for staff who are not only good at making excellent sandwiches and are hygiene conscious but we are also try hard to employ listening, caring, smiling people who say thank you and have a sense of fun. We try to encourage people to stay with the company for as long as possible. People will definitely notice a difference in the speed and quality of our service and the attitude of our staff'. The family connection is assured in the shape of Jenny, Neil's daughter, who represents the fifth generation. She has worked in the Ladybarn shop and factory during her school holidays and at Christmas and Easter.

Martins' first new bakery shop of the third millennium was the former Trifles in Droylsden, an event which marked the return of the firm to Droylsden after a 22 year absence.

Perhaps the last word about Martins should be the firm's motto ' Made today - sold today' a philosophy which no doubts goes a long way to explaining the firm's continuing high reputation and award winning performance as the best sandwich maker in Britain.

Above: *One of the cheques given to the Booth Hall Children's Hospital for the proceeds from the Bobby the Bear gingerbread biscuits.*
Below left: *Richard Martin junior with his sons, Neil and Ian in 1991.*
Below: *Martins' Cheetham Hill shop.*

> *The Central Library, at its opening, was the largest public library in Britain*

Aerial views

At least two aeroplanes must have been flying over Central Manchester at this moment in time in 1934, and one of them captured this splendid shot of the distinctively circular Central Library, in the year of its opening. The most important city centre building constructed since the Town Hall, 70 years earlier, it had been designed by Vincent Harris, and the foundation stone had been laid in 1930. The beauty of the building lies in its Classic simplicity of style, and at its opening it was the largest public library in Britain. The rotunda of the reference section is clearly visible in this aerial view, and the Library also houses a theatre, a shop, and a cafe. The site under clearance towards the top of the photograph was earmarked for the Town Hall Extension, and when the Library was officially declared open by King George V in July 1934, he laid the foundation stone for the Extension, which was completed in 1937. To the right of the Library, facing its front entrance, is St Peter's Square containing the Cenotaph, designed by Lutyens. As if to complete a geometry lesson, the bottom of the photograph shows the massive triangular shape of the Midland. Once a flagship railway hotel, it now rejoices under the name of the Holiday Inn Crowne Plaza Midland.

Belle Vue Gardens, as pictured in 1930, had grown enormously from the small-scale operation that first opened its gates in 1836. An imaginative entrepreneur, John Jennison, took a trial lease for six months on 35 acres of land on Hyde Road, with a view to creating show gardens and a small zoo. He then took out a 99 year lease and the Belle Vue story had begun. The zoo quickly expanded, and other attractions such as a maze were added. Not all were successful - the racecourse was closed down after 1848 - but by the time of his death, in 1867, John Jennison

had gone a long way towards making Belle Vue one of Manchester's favourite 'playgrounds'. The boating lake was opened in 1843, and this is clearly visible towards the top of the picture, with its island. They were often known as Firework Lake and Firework Island because of the impressive displays of pyrotechnics that were put on there for many years. These great annual events grew in scope until they took the form of dramatic plays with lots of thrilling noise and action. More thrills could be found on some of Belle Vue's exciting rides, one of which can be seen towards the bottom.

Manchester Central Library: Local Studies Unit

Manchester Central Library: Local Studies Unit

Left: *Victoria Station, towards the top, is the first focus point in this picture. The station opened in 1844, operating both for the London & North Western and the Lancashire & Yorkshire Railways. The former, however, built its own Exchange Station in 1884, linked to Victoria by 'the longest platform in the world'. Exchange Station closed in 1969, but Victoria lives on, perhaps its best known feature being the tiled wall map of the Lancashire & Yorkshire Railway. From the top right-hand corner of the station Corporation Street follows a straight line down the photograph, as was the intention of its designers, who wanted to create a direct route between the Market Place and Ducie Bridge around 1850. The tall tower of the Cooperative Insurance Society is a prominent landmark at top right, and much of this area is occupied by CWS buildings. It is fairly easy to pick out Manchester Cathedral, to the far left, and above this is Chetham's, the internationally renowned Music School, along with the equally famous Chetham's Library. The Chetham's site is rich in history, being the former home of the old Manchester Grammar School (founded in 1515) for 40 poor boys.*

Above: *An eye-catching feature of this aerial shot of Belle Vue in 1937 is the oval shape of the speedway stadium to the left. The colourful and flamboyant Johnny Hoskins brought speedway to Britain from Australia in 1928, and the Belle Vue Aces were quick to appear on the scene. The first meeting was held at the Greyhound Stadium in 1928, but speedway got a separate venue of its own from March 1929. Few sports can match speedway for the thrills and spills that can be packed into short bursts of action. Once experienced, who can ever forget that tremendous howl of noise as the tapes go up, or that distinctive smell of high octane fuel hanging in the air? The Aces certainly had their stars, from Frank ('Red Devil') Varey riding in the 1930s, to Peter Collins who won the World Championship in 1976. The early part of this decade was a great one for the Aces, who won the British League Championship in three successive seasons and the Knockout Cup in 1973. A stock car meeting in 1987 was the last event to be held at the stadium before it was sold to British Car Auctions. However, Peter Collins re-established the Aces at the Greyhound Racing Stadium in 1988.*

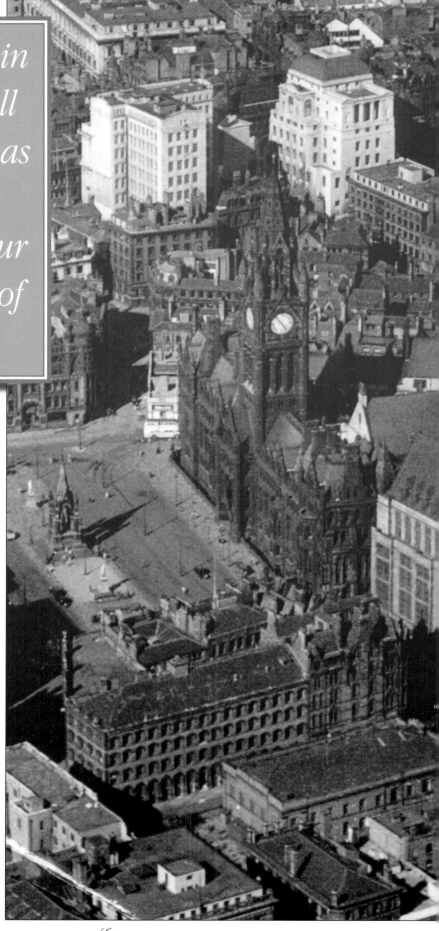

The huge bell in the Town Hall clock tower was named 'Big Abel' in honour of the Mayor of the time

The focus of this aerial shot of the 1950s is the cluster of buildings and squares that make up the heart of the city. Even from this altitude the 286 feet high clock tower of the impressive Town Hall is a dominating feature. The building, designed by Alfred Waterhouse and completed in 1877, is a fine example of Victorian architecture. It was the dynamism of the mayor of the day, Abel Heywood, which got the Town Hall underway, and the huge bell which strikes the hour in the clock tower was named 'Big Abel' in his honour. The Town Hall had not undergone stone cleaning at this stage, and so the contrast between its smoke stained exterior and that of its extension, to the immediate right, is all the more marked. The extension was completed in 1937, to complement the building of the beautifully circular Central Library in 1934. The equally distinctive triangle of the Midland Hotel stands just below the Library. Faced with terra cotta, which was supposed to offer more resistance to the soot in the air, the Hotel was opened in 1903. With 400 bedrooms, each with a telephone, it was the height of luxury, containing a Palm Court, a theatre and Rose Garden on the roof.

Left: World War II bombings left their mark on Manchester for some time after the conflict ended in 1945, in this case in the form of a strange triangular shape to the top left. This was the site of the former Victoria Buildings, burned to the ground in 1940, but laid out as pleasant gardens in the photograph. The same raid put an incendiary bomb through the roof of the Royal Exchange, whose tower seems to project into the garden triangle. Fortunately there was no permanent damage to this magnificent building, which since the 1870s had provided a commercial centre for the cotton trade as an expanded version of the previous Exchange. The Cathedral, towards the top, is bounded to the right by yet another triangle - that formed by the buildings of the Corn (Produce) Exchange. A popular meeting spot for Manchester grocers, the first Corn Exchange was opened in 1837, and the existing one was completed in 1903. Trade and barter took place in the central area, under the glass and steel canopy, whilst shops and offices occupied the triangle of buildings. The Cathedral is clearly visible, and a church has stood on this site since Norman times. Cathedral status was gained in 1847, but there has been extensive building and re-building since the Middle Ages.

Below: Central Station, towards bottom middle, imposes its presence on this photograph, the curve of its arched roof being unmistakable. The opening of this terminus station, in 1880, allowed the Cheshire Lines Railway to compete with the companies running out of Victoria (and later Exchange) Stations for the lucrative Liverpool traffic. Central Station was closed in 1969, to reopen in 1986 as the successful exhibition centre, G-Mex. The striking steel and glass main entrance, containing the old railway clock, conserves the elegant Victorian design of Central Station, as does the magnificent single-span arched roof. Just above the station are two more landmarks that are easily identifiable through their shapes - the triangle of the Midland Hotel and the circle of the Central Library, with the Town Hall just beyond. The Midland was the great railway hotel that served Central Station when it had passed into the part ownership of the London, Midland and Scottish Railway. A little covered walkway used to run between the Station and the Hotel to protect customers from the weather. Mosley Street can be followed up from St Peter's Square, to the right of the Midland, and into Piccadilly, where the Rylands Building stands out prominently. To the left, Deansgate cuts a long straight line up towards the distant Cathedral.

The People's War

In April 1939 Manchester Education Authority compiled a register of prospective evacuees in the event of war. The names of around 129,000 school and pre-school children were put forward by parents, and 4000 expectant mothers and disabled adults were added to the list. Detailed plans were drawn up and a rehearsal was held on August 28th. What a poignant scene as the reality of impending war is brought home to Manchester. The date is September 1st 1939, two days before the official outbreak of war with Germany, and the evacuation of the young and the vulnerable is well underway. A fleet of buses stands by to ferry the evacuees to all the city and suburban railway stations. It must have seemed beyond belief to the male bystanders, who were probably fathers or husbands, that their children and some of their womenfolk were departing from them to destinations that at first were kept secret. No doubt there are plenty of Mancunians who still remember the tearful (and fearful) farewells of that day, although the younger children probably regarded it as a great adventure at first. Identification labels were firmly attached to all, and personal possessions were packed into whatever was handy. The two little girls at the back of the queue look in danger of being pulled over backwards by the huge packs on their backs! What is on view was part of a well-planned operation. As war had become increasingly likely from Spring 1939 Manchester, along with other industrial areas, had been seen as a prime target for air raids. Evacuation schemes were being laid down from that point.

Manchester Central Library: Local Studies Unit

The faces of these young girls are cheerful enough, but these were grim and frightening times in 1939. The photograph shows the spartan interior of the air raid shelter attached to Sharston Senior School and, in spite of the smiles, conditions appear to be cramped and claustrophobic. Massive civilian casualties from German air raids was one of the government's major fears at the outbreak of war in 1939. Civil Defence organisations were already in place by 1938, including Air Raid Precaution (ARP) units for every area. Raids were expected to come mainly at night, but what if attacks came by day when people were at work or school? Hence air raid shelters were constructed at schools and factories, along with public ones. Those at Piccadilly were originally constructed out of sandbags, to be replaced by brick and concrete in 1941. More could be found in Albert Square, and the Town Hall had shelter accommodation for over 2,000. The Victoria Street arches were converted into shelters. The schoolgirls in the photograph are dutifully clutching the little square boxes containing their gas masks. Gas attack was the greatest fear of all, and as early as 1938 the government had distributed 38 million gas masks.

On the home front

Older Mancunians will still remember that mournful sound - the wail of the air raid siren. Then it would be the dash to the nearest public air raid shelter, or to the Anderson shelter in the garden or maybe staying put in the house and taking a chance. Another sound from those splintered nights of World War II was that heavy throb of bomb-laden German aircraft overhead. This was the nightmare that came true, for even whilst gas masks were being distributed and shelters built in the months before the outbreak of war, a sense of unreality persisted. Therefore it may have been with a sense of shock that Mancunians witnessed, on September 1st 1939, long 'crocodiles' of schoolchildren on the streets of Manchester, heading for railway stations or for buses that would take them there. The great evacuation was on, and throughout that first day 46,274 children left Manchester, heading for safer areas such as Cheshire and Derbyshire. Meanwhile the preparations went on for the expected onslaught from the air. The public was warned that gas masks had to be carried at all times. A total blackout was imposed during the hours of darkness, leading to a spate of accidents in the early

months. White lines had to be painted on lamp posts and along the edges of kerbs. Cheap blackout paper for windows was available at Boots for one shilling and sixpence (7p) a roll. 'Put that light out', became the common cry of the air raid wardens after dark. Public shelters were built at Piccadilly and Albert Square. The Town Hall had shelter accommodation for over 2,000. And still no bombs fell; the 'phoney war' was on; some evacuees drifted back home. Almost a year after the war had begun, in the summer of 1940, scattered bombs began to fall. But it was not until the so-called Christmas 'Blitz' of 1940 that the full reality of aerial attack came home to Manchester. Two nights of heavy bombing reduced large parts of the centre to rubble, with fires raging uncontrollably . Victoria Buildings, the Free Trade Hall and warehouses in Piccadilly were just some of the buildings totally destroyed. The Whitsun 'Blitz' of 1941 was less intense, but is remembered for the tragedy of the 14 nurses killed by a direct hit on the Salford Royal. The war on the Home Front cost the lives of 559 Mancunians and left the city physically scarred for many years to come.

The date is September 1st 1939 and the evacuation of the young and the vulnerable is well underway.

Manchester Central Library: Local Studies Unit

M.C.C.D
Salvage
Appeal
Deposit for
Old
Keys,
Trinkets
Etc,

Manchester Central Library: Local Studies Unit

Left: This patriotic lady is doing her best for the war effort as she is about to pop something into the collecting box on Oxford Street in 1940. She was contributing something to the Salvage Appeal which, in this particular instance, was inviting gifts of smaller items such as old keys and trinkets. The lady's outfit is very '1940s', right down to her seamed stockings, and another indication of the war years is the white-striped lamp standard, an aid to navigation during the blackout. Fighting a successful war required a tremendous collective effort, both from the armed forces and the civilians. Collecting salvage was just one of the areas in which civilians could contribute, particularly in view of the shortages being imposed by the German 'U'-boat campaign against British ships. Anything that could be re-used was gathered in, from metal park railings to kitchen waste for pig swill. Paper, textiles, glass, bottle tops and even ashes had their salvage value. Aluminium saucepans were of great value for aircraft production. 'Send Your Pans Flying', was the slogan, '5,000 make a fighter and 25,000 make a bomber'. In the first year of war, Manchester collected 8,151 tons of metal and 4,029 tons of paper, worth collectively £40,310, excluding salvage from blitzed buildings.

Above: The imposing frontage of the Northern Assurance Buildings makes an impressive backdrop to this wartime scene. Albert Square had seen many spectacles in its history, but it is doubtful if a tank had ever rumbled across its cobbles before, and the large crowd that has gathered bears witness to the interest aroused in Manchester by this unusual event. It was all part of the Tanks for Attack Campaign of 1941, which was a nationwide government venture to raise awareness, increase solidarity and, perhaps most of all, raise money. Wars can be ruinously expensive, and with Britain engaged in a fight to the death with Germany, money had to be raised in every way possible. Apart from the Tanks for Attack Campaign, other huge wartime drives were War Weapons Week, Wings for Victory and Salute the Soldier. The general pattern was a week of events revolving around the central theme, always with the aim of persuading people to buy War Bonds, or in other ways invest in the government. Warship Week in 1942, for example, included parades, demonstrations of unarmed combat and a large model of 'HMS Nelson' displayed in Piccadilly. The week raised the staggering sum of £12,500,000 from Mancunians, an average of almost £2.75 per head.

Manchester Central Library: Local Studies Unit

Above: The townscape behind Parker Street, Piccadilly, was changed dramatically and permanently by the heavy German air raid of December 23rd/24th 1940. The heaps of rubble show all that was left of the great warehouses of Staines Inlaid Linoleum; Peel, Watson & Co and J Templeton & Co. The huge and fierce blaze spread round into Portland Street, fanned by a strong wind. Manchester Fire Brigade fought at full stretch to contain this and other fires. Surrounding districts sent in 3,400 extra men to help, but the fracturing of the water main from Longdendale reservoirs hindered the firefighters. In the end, the only way to control the inferno of the Parker Street warehouses was to create fire-breaks by dynamiting nearby buildings. Churches and hospitals were also badly hit by the Christmas 'Blitz', including the Royal Eye Hospital and the Jewish Hospital. A parachute mine seriously damaged Manchester Cathedral. Private homes felt the weight of the bombs also, and in the Whitsun raid of 1941, 14 nurses were killed at Salford Royal Infirmary. Many Mancunians will still remember these dark days when 559 of their number lost their lives through bombing and 572 were seriously injured. Raids totally destroyed 389 of their houses, with 1,562 so badly damaged that they had to be demolished.

Manchester Central Library: Local Studies Unit

Below centre: The smoking ruins of what had once been a part of Cannon Street presented a grim sight after the Christmas 'Blitz' of 1940. The fact that the expected air onslaught on Britain did not materialise immediately, lulled people into a false sense of security. In fact, so few bombs fell on the country between September 1939 and July 1940, that this period was dubbed the 'phoney war' and, tragically in some cases, many parents brought their evacuated children back home to the cities. The first bomb on Manchester fell in the Salford area on July 29th 1940. There were a few more scattered raids, but nothing could have prepared Mancunians for the events of late 1940. At 6.40 pm on December 22nd incendiaries were dropped in the area of Albert Square, and the light provided by the fires allowed the Luftwaffe to pound the city for the next five hours. The pattern was followed the following night, incendiaries followed by high explosive bombs, 288 in total over the two nights. Apart from Cannon Street, there was heavy damage in Piccadilly, the Old Shambles and the Market Place. The Victoria Buildings were destroyed, as well as the famous Free Trade Hall. Part of the Exchange Station disappeared and a landmine fell on Platform 16 of Victoria Station.

Manchester Central Library: Local Studies Unit

Right: Royal visits to Manchester are part of a long tradition. Queen Victoria visited in 1851, 1857 (to visit the Arts Treasures Exhibition at Old Trafford) and 1894, adding a touch of colour and pageantry to the daily life of the city. How much more such occasions are appreciated in wartime, when ordinary people see a royal visit as some recognition of the sacrifices, hardship and danger they are undergoing. This particular photograph is dated 1945, and although this may not be completely accurate, it is almost certainly a wartime occasion. King George VI wears RAF uniform, and other military dress is visible. The ladies standing against the wall, to the left, are dressed in 1940s fashion, and could the middle one be desperately winding on the film of her Brownie box camera? Taking quick snaps was not quite so easy in those days! Whatever the year, the tiny tots with their patriotic flags make this a happy scene. Queen Elizabeth, as always looks relaxed and at ease. She is wearing her famous silver fox furs, although the Lord Mayor seems to be upstaging her in this department. George VI cuts a rather more reserved figure, but this was his temperament, and people respected his quiet but resolute qualities during World War II.

Below: It's all over - at last! The happy faces in the packed crowd thronging Albert Square say it all on that landmark day, May 8th 1945, 'VE Day'. Victory in Europe meant the end of six long years of blackouts, gas masks and the air raids that had brought death and destruction. The official ceremonies began with a service in the Cathedral at 11.30 am. In the afternoon the Lord Mayor made the official announcement from the Town Hall, and the 44 flags of the founder members of the United Nations were unfurled. This was followed by a relay of King George VI's broadcast to the dense crowds. Some of the flags can be seen on the photograph, but perhaps the most heartfelt message was the tribute to Britain's Allies emblazoned across the huge Victory emblem at the back. No doubt the USA, the USSR and the British Empire and Commonwealth were the ones being saluted. To stand on top of the air raid shelters, rather than crouch within them, seemed almost like a symbolic gesture - freedom from fear. Then the fun began in the streets of Manchester with singing, dancing and parties. Bonfires blazed in parks whilst a decorated tram and an illuminated bus toured the streets. Effigies of Hitler swung from more than one lamp-post or factory gate.

Manchester Central Library: Local Studies Unit

Above: Two contrasting sides of 'VJ Day' are neatly summed up in one image. If a picture is worth 1,000 words then this is a fine example of the old saying. The Union Jack in the background speaks of patriotism and celebration - the war was finally over. The long bread queue shows that in some ways nothing had changed on August 15th 1945. The official end of the war would not miraculously fill shops with food - the shortages would continue. There are some cheerful smiles for the camera, and a repetition of the Shudehill Fights - the bread riots of 1756 - was unlikely, but these Mancunians must have been feeling a little fed up. Food shortages had caused rationing to be introduced early in 1940. Unless people had access to the 'black market', they had learned to live with restrictions such as four ounces (112 grammes) of bacon, two ounces (56 grammes) of tea and half an egg per week. Now that the war was over, better things were expected, but devastated countries across the world could not immediately produce them. In fact bread went on ration for the first time in 1946! Saccharine tablets and dried egg powder still had some years to run, and elements of rationing remained until 1954.

Above right: According to the 'Manchester Guardian', the news that the war in Europe had ended was something of an anti-climax on May 8th 1945, for rumours to that effect had been in the air for some time. There does not seem much of the anti-climactic about this particular celebration in one of Manchester's suburbs. 'VE' Day is being greeted by a rousing march along the cobbles, accompanied by a sing-song. A real effort has gone into decorating the streets, and it looks as if it is an air raid shelter that has been embellished with the huge Union Jack. Not to have to cower inside that shelter any more was more than reason enough for rejoicing! Scenes of this kind were being enacted elsewhere, and the children of Aked Street, Ardwick had the treat of watching old Chaplin films at midnight. Albert Square was a seething mass of people by the time that the Lord Mayor made the official announcement from the steps of the Town Hall in the afternoon. The bands played; people danced and sang; there was only one problem - there wasn't much to celebrate with. Food was still rationed; there was not a cigarette to be bought, and the pubs were soon sold out of their limited supplies of beer and spirits.

Patriotism, relief and sheer exuberance make up the ingredients of this celebration at Rosamond Grove, Chorlton-on-Medlock, on August 15th 1945. It was 'VJ Day', the surrender of Japan finally ending the conflict that had torn the world (and families) apart for six years. A portrait of Churchill above a giant Union Jack looks benignly down at the dancing and revels that were going to continue for two days. The joy at Rosamond Grove was mirrored right across the city as Mancunians 'let their hair down'. The central area began to fill with singing and dancing crowds from midnight on August 14th, long before the Lord Mayor made the official announcement from the Town Hall at 10 am the following day. Amidst the celebrations there were also services of thanksgiving in churches, and indeed the end of the war engendered in some more of a reflective than a celebratory mood. After all, the war had seen some Mancunians parted from their loved ones forever. Others had not heard from their menfolk literally for years, and had no idea if they were dead or alive. Also, those who had seen film of the awesome atomic power used against Japan could only wonder what this might mean for the future.

Transport and Piccadilly go hand-in-hand, although perhaps today's visitors to Manchester are more inclined to associate this historic area with the main line railway station. However, the link between Piccadilly Gardens and transport goes back a good deal further than the railway age, but at the same time the Gardens also manifest the most recent development in the shape of the MetroLink tram system. Cars and buses are the themes of this 1957 picture, and a good deal of pleasure can be derived from spotting the different models of cars on show, some of which might rekindle a few memories amongst those who first nervously touched the controls of a car in that era. The number of vehicles on the road was rising rapidly in 1957, along with parking problems, and so these car owners might well have felt grateful for the huge open spaces available on the Parker Street side of Piccadilly. These had come about courtesy of the Luftwaffe, and the destruction of the line of large warehouses that had stood there in the December 'Blitz' of 1940. However, the diggers and wagons were not creating more car parking space. The work in hand was the extension of the bus station.

Below: A few months later in 1957 and the job is done, with new bays for the buses and the cars in retreat. The line of buildings in the background, along Mosley Street, would present much the same image today, with Lewis's still in occupation. However, the virtues of 'Mother's Pride' bread are no longer boldly displayed, and Yates the Seedsmen (as advertised on the shop canopies) have gone. The Halifax Building Society sign fills the length of the white building, but this organisation is now to be found elsewhere in Piccadilly. As for the cars, the expanses of parking space abruptly disappeared in 1960, for the bombsites were earmarked for other things. Slowly, and perhaps to the astonishment of Mancunians, the Piccadilly Plaza Suite unfolded itself. Have any structures in the city caused so much controversy as the Hotel Piccadilly with the Plaza Cafe below, the Sunley Tower office block and Bernard House, topped with its strange 'wings'? In all likelihood, the designers of this post-war era were trying to break away from the past and create a 'brave new world', something that symbolised progress. But in totally rejecting the past, they created something completely out of sympathy with the older buildings around Piccadilly.

Wheels of time

Above: 'Fly BEA', is the invitation which beckons down Mosley Street in 1957 and flying is one of the few forms of transportation which has not been associated with Piccadilly down the ages. We are familiar with the cars, buses and trams of Piccadilly, but even before John Greenwood started his horse-drawn bus service in 1824, the area was the centre of a thriving coaching industry. Quite close to the spot where the bus station is pictured, coaches plied their trade from the White Bear and the Bridgewater Arms, both converted into inns in the late 18th century. The dark red and black coaches, each pulled by four horses, offered a nationwide service, and in 1801 the White Bear took pride in its 'London Flying Machine', which did the journey in only two days! The name Mosley Street is a reminder that Piccadilly was once a pleasant rural area of estates owned by prominent Manchester families such as the Levers and the Mosleys. Lever Street runs into another corner of Piccadilly. It was Sir Oswald Mosley who granted the rights for the building of the Royal Infirmary on part of his land in 1755. Demolished in 1908, the Infirmary's legacy was Piccadilly Gardens, a slight hint of the area's pastoral past.

Above right: The various forms of transport represented by this shot of Piccadilly Gardens in 1937 are a reminder of just how much this area is associated with the comings and goings of the human throng. As early as 1824 John Greenwood was running a horse omnibus service between Market Street and Pendleton, the first one of its kind in Britain. Steel rails offered a smoother ride than bumpy cobbles, and so from 1877 horse-drawn trams were 'flying' about Manchester at breakneck speeds of six to seven miles per hour, carrying up to 40 passengers each. As there were no direct cross-town links, all routes led to Piccadilly - the age of congestion had begun! The next step forward was for the Manchester Carriage and Tramways Company to introduce electrification to their trams, and this began in 1901. The social effect of cheap public transport was to allow working people to move out of the overcrowded central areas to more pleasant suburbs. With the gradual replacement of trams, firstly by electric trolley buses and later by motor buses, it seemed like the end of an era when the last tram ran in 1949. However, full circle of a kind was reached when the gentle hoot of the Metrolink tram service was heard in the streets from 1992.

Manchester Central Library: Local Studies Unit

Right: It was May 1959 when this scene was captured along Warwick Road, and the buses waiting to ferry the football supporters away after the game have that 1950s look about them, as does the advertisement on the first one - 'Players Please'. This was a difficult time for Manchester United for it had struggled its way out of immediate post-war difficulties, only to be devastated by the Munich tragedy in 1958. Manchester United emerged from World War II without a manager, in debt to the tune of £70,000, and unable to play at Old Trafford because of the damage caused by German bombing in 1941. In fact, United played their home games at Maine Road until 1949. The first step on the road forward was the appointment of a genius of a manager, Matt Busby. It was he who created that wonderful team which won the League Championship in 1952, 1956 and 1957, and the young stars known as the 'Busby Babes' were poised to achieve so much more. Then, on a February night in 1958, came that terrible disaster at Munich Airport. Eight players died - Byrne, Colman, Jones, Edwards, Pegg, Taylor, Bent and Whelan - and two more survived but had played their last match. The rebuilding had to start all over again.

Bottom: Perhaps some older readers may have witnessed these astonishing scenes in November 1946. If it appears as if an angry crowd is attempting to pull a bus driver from his cab, then this is exactly the case, and it was the result of a seemingly minor dispute escalating into a strike which involved over 5,000 bus workers. In November 1946 a Manchester Corporation bus driver was dismissed after being reported for speeding by a pedestrian. The bus drivers and conductors at the Queen's Road depot went on strike, demanding their colleague's reinstatement, and by November 18th over 5,000 were on strike as other depots joined in. As the photograph shows, the dispute turned ugly when the Transport Department tried to run a 'skeleton' service manned by volunteers - mainly students. Outside the Princess Road depot fighting broke out when 200 pickets tried forcibly to remove volunteer student drivers from their cabs. In later incidents the same day, strikers threw bricks through bus windows and allegedly tried to overturn a bus! Many thousands of foot weary Mancunians had to trudge back and forth to work until the dispute was settled on November 21st. The students of 1946 were a different breed from the left-wingers of the 1960s, who would probably have been on the picket lines!

Manchester Central Library: Local Studies Unit

The flower beds of Piccadilly are seen to some advantage here, and appear to be in good shape. Plenty of people are sitting and simply enjoying the sights, and perhaps the scents. This 1957 photograph was taken from the vantage point of the BBC building. In 1926, on the corner of Piccadilly and Oldham Street, a Woolworth's store had been opened on the site of the old Albion Hotel. Another new building next door saw its upper floors become home to the BBC in Manchester. Radio broadcasting in the city had begun in 1922 at Trafford Park, basing itself at Piccadilly in 1928.

There it stayed until new premises were opened on Oxford Road in 1975. For anyone gazing out of the BBC windows in 1957, the great open spaces beyond Parker Street would have been a reminder that World War II had ended little more than a decade earlier. Those spaces had been occupied by the great warehouses of Staines Inlaid Linoleum and Peel, Watson & Co, along with J Templeton & Co, until the Manchester 'Blitz' of late December 1940 had caused the raging infernos that destroyed them. The luxury of acres of open car parking had not long to last, for the building of the Piccadilly Plaza Suite was to begin in 1960.

A scene of incredible confusion greets the eye as cars, wagons, tankers, buses, taxis and pedestrians slug it out. The date - 1953; the place - the junction of Market Street with Cross and Corporation Streets, traditionally one of Manchester's busiest spots in those days. The policeman on the corner looks as if he ought to be going on point duty, but is perhaps thinking better of it. As for the pedestrians, the refuge islands have been very aptly named in this case. Such problems were common to the centre of the city, particularly at peak times, and this was before the real rise of mass car ownership. Heavy vehicles seem to be the main culprits, and it was to ease such congestion as this that the Mancunian Way was built. The 'highway in the sky' on its concrete pillars was quite a wonder at first. More radical developments, however, were to take place in the area of the photograph. These 1953 shoppers would scarcely recognise the Market Street of today, pedestrianised from High Street and disappearing under the cover of the Arndale Centre at the approach to this junction. This huge scheme saw the creation of the great Arndale wall between 1972 and 1976, stretching as far as Cannon Street.

The massive foundations of the Mayes Street Trench dominate this photograph of 1940. An air raid shelter was under construction at Mayes Street, close to Miller Street, and it is quite likely that it was for the use of the employees of the Cooperative Wholesale Society, whose premises can be seen to the rear. It was an impressively large project judging by the quantities of materials and equipment on view, but doubtless speed was the watchword, for German bombs had begun to fall on Manchester by 1940. Public air raid shelters could be found at Piccadilly and Albert Square, and even the tunnel through which the former Manchester and Salford Canal ran had been adapted for air raid purposes. In addition shelters were built at schools, and firms were encouraged to protect their employees in the same way. Of course households could have their own 'luxurious' private accommodation in the shape of Anderson Shelters. Containing bunks for six, these were dug deeply into gardens, leaving only a semi-circle of corrugated metal above ground, reinforced by turf and sandbags. By the end of 1939, Manchester Air Raid Precaution reported that the city had 30,000 such shelters, along with 3,698 domestic surface shelters.

Earning a crust

The perfect blend assured for over a century

When it comes to making a pot of tea 'Brooke Bond' is one of the world's most popular household names. Yet Brooke Bond has its origins firmly rooted in Manchester; it was in 1869 that Arthur Brooke first opened a shop in the city selling his own blends of tea, coffee and sugar. There never was a Mr Bond: according to Arthur Brooke 'it seemed to sound so well' that he simply added it to his own name to complete the company's title!

Arthur Brooke was born in 1845 above the family shop in George Street, Ashton-under-Lyne; his father, Charles Brooke, was a tea wholesaler. Despite his father's trade young Arthur entered the cotton industry - though soon leaving that business when, at the age of 19, the mill in which he was a partner failed due to the disruption of supplies of raw cotton during the American Civil War. Arthur then went to Liverpool and later London working for Peek Bros & Winch, a wholesale tea company, before eventually returning home to help his father whose business was in decline.

Arthur Brooke began his own business at the age of only 24 using £400 saved from his share of profits from his father's firm. His first shop was at 29 Market Street, Manchester. Above the shop he hung his now famous, if inaccurate, sign 'Brooke, Bond & Co Limited'.

Arthur revolutionised the trade, selling tea, coffee and sugar for cash only; that policy enabled him to keep prices low and quality high as his business was not hampered by credit and debts.

Rather than sell tea loose from chests Arthur Brooke developed his own quality blends by mixing various teas to give a more consistent taste.

Above left: *Arthur Brooke, founder of the company.*
Below: *29 Market Street.*

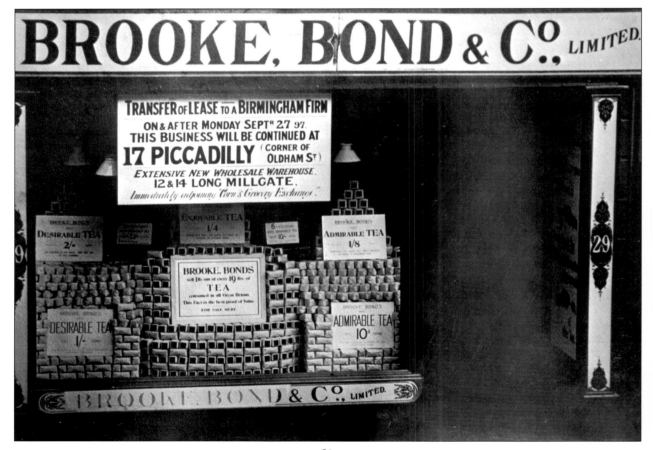

This became the very principle which would later lead Brooke Bond to create PG Tips and other favourite blended brands. Tea was sold in ½ lb and 1 lb paper bags; in the shop window Arthur put a mechanical wooden figure, known as Jack, which both advertised his wares and attracted passing custom.

In order to guard against competitors imitating his products each tea packet was printed with 'Brooke Bond & Co' in Arthur's famous flowing script. This not only made the product instantly identifiable but for over a century also served as a trademark - since although it was not a criminal offence to imitate a competitor's product forging his signature certainly was.

Arthur Brooke quickly gained a reputation amongst both the public and grocers, some of whom began to ask if they could buy his tea in bulk. Business flourished. More shops were soon opened in Liverpool, Leeds and Bradford. In 1872 Arthur moved to London establishing a warehouse at 129 Whitechapel High Street which became the company offices.

Despite inevitable set backs, including the failure of two shops in London and the poor management of the Liverpool shop run by Arthur's brother-in-law Arthur Bushell, nevertheless by the age of 30 Arthur Brooke was making £5,000 a year. Arthur had become a rich man. In 1875 he married a naval captain's daughter Alice Catherine Young and set up home in Stonebridge Park, Willesden.

In the late 1870s a trade depression hit Britain and the tea business ran into serious trouble; shops in Scotland had to be sold and Arthur had to sell his house in Willesden and move to a smaller property at Bedford Park. The tide turned when Arthur recognised the potential of selling his tea in bulk, wholesale, direct to grocers - though on a cash with order basis. Becoming both retail and wholesale suppliers of tea enabled the business to survive and by 1887 Arthur was able to buy a house in Kensington and a country house near Dorking.

Above: *St Dunstan's Saleroom.*

In 1892 Brooke Bond and Company became a limited company with a share capital of £150,000. The business was by now largely wholesale with the advantage that unlike other firms the business did not need to employ travellers or 'reps' but instead relied on its fine reputation to obtain new and repeat business.

Competition and rivalry demanded a cheaper blend of tea however. In 1898 Brooke Bond launched a 'True Tea' at 10d (4p) a pound. In 1899 Gerald Brooke, Arthur's eldest son, left school to join the business and rapidly found himself packing tea at Boar Lane in Leeds. It was a baptism of fire. Despite the hard work, however, there was never a shortage of people willing to work for Brooke Bond: Arthur was a generous employer being one of the first to give his workers bonuses and to reduce the working day to eight hours.

Arthur was also generous to his customers; in 1899 for example the year of Queen Victoria's 80th birthday he gave all regular customers over the age of 80 one pound of free tea.

The company widened its horizons considerably when at the turn of the new century it looked to add the Indian market to its overseas interests. In 1902 that expansion was realised with the winning of the contract to supply tea to the Delhi Durbar.

By 1904 Arthur Brooke was looking forward to retirement and to handing the reins to his son Gerald. Almost inevitably misfortune struck: in 1905 a serious misjudgement of the Calcutta market resulted in disastrously reduced profits. Arthur was forced to delay his retirement and to recruit additional help to strengthen the sales and purchasing side of the business.

Gerald Brooke eventually succeeded his father as company chairman, but not until 1910. The first years of his chairmanship saw the start of mechanisation as well as experimentation with automated production and packing machines; Brooke Bond also began using motor vans in place of horse drawn vehicles to distribute its goods.

Following the outbreak of the first world war in 1914 tea imports were curtailed by the government. Gerald Brooke instantly turned over to coffee and sales were healthy. Public outcry however soon led to a reversal of government policy and the restriction on tea imports was relaxed.

With the end of the Great War in 1918 tea sales continued to grow and outpaced existing production facilities in London and Manchester.

Below: *Early delivery methods.*

In 1922 a new purpose built tea-blending and packing factory was constructed in Trafford Park which remains there to this day. Sadly Arthur Brooke did not live to see that new development: he died on 13th April 1918 leaving a considerable fortune.

In the 1930s tea was often sold for its claimed medicinal properties. One blend was promoted through a campaign aimed at doctors and nurses on the strength of its properties as an aid to digestion. Some early adverts contained references to the qualities of 'digestive tea' or 'pre-gestive tea'.

Legal objections were soon made to these unsubstantiated medical claims and to the use of the word 'digestive' in association with tea. John Peel, Brooke Bond's home sales director, countered this challenge by inventing the name 'Pre-Gest-tea'. Bulk packets of Pre-Gest tea bore the letters 'PG' and the blend soon became known in the trade as simply 'PG Tips' as only the tips of the tea bush were plucked. This soon became a brand name, one which has survived to the present day.

In 1955 PG Tips became the feature of an amusing and unusual advertising campaign which was to become one of the most successful and long running in the history of television.

It was Bill Barter of Spottiswoods advertising agency who suggested that chimpanzees be used in a television commercial.

Chimps had a long association with tea due to the long-running 'Chimps Tea Party' at London Zoo which was a major attraction for both children and adults.

The first two television commercials produced for Brooke Bond were 'Stately Home' and 'Chimps Tea Party' featuring the Marquis troupe of chimps trained for cabaret by Gene Detroy. That first ever Brooke Bond TV commercial was broadcast on Christmas Day 1956 and featured the chimps sipping delicately from bone china cups in an elegant country mansion.

Top: A Trojan van.
Above: Arthur Brooke's statue in the Trafford Centre.

A further series featured chimps from Billy Smart's Circus. The popularity of those commercials exceeded all expectations with voices provided by such famous names as Peter Sellers, Bruce Forsythe and Bob Monkhouse. Very quickly the commercials became so popular that the chimps were in great demand for public appearances.

Probably the most famous and successful troupe of chimps used in the advertisements were now discovered and signed up by Brooke Bond. These chimps were owned and trained by Molly Badham and, as well as appearing in television commercials, made public appearances around the country opening super-markets and new stores. They even attended a Brooke Bond staff party to mark the retirement of Lillian Bristow as advertising manager; there Johnny, Judy, Sam and Rosie proved popular and charming guests, with Rosie demonstrating a particular liking for gin and orange and almond icing!

The success of the PG Chimp commercials certainly helped Brooke Bond sell more tea. By 1957 the adver-tising budget had reached £680,000 but that high cost was more than offset by the increase in sales: the company could now say that one in every four families in Britain was drinking Brooke Bond tea.

As well as opening supermarkets the chimps appeared live at Saturday morning film shows staged by the company's own projection units which during weekdays and evenings presented documentaries to schools and institutions all over the country.

Probably the best remembered advert of the series is 'Mr Shifter' the saga of the removal firm and piano on the stairs. That advert has been on television more times than any other commercial earning itself a place in the Guinness Book of Records.

Below: *The premises at Trafford Park Road.*

the increasingly collectable and valuable set of egg cups featuring Sergeant Chimp, Navvy Chimp, Mr Shifter and Cyril the Cyclist, all from the early 1970s.

Today the Brooke Bond Tea Company is part of Van Den Bergh Foods Ltd. Van Den Bergh Foods is Unilever's largest food company in the UK employing over 3,000 at eight major sites. The factory in Trafford Park employs around 420 people manufacturing and producing tea products including PG Tips, Brooke Bond D, Scottish Blend and Choicest Blend. The secret of the firm's continuing success still lies in the expert selection and blending of teas so that each brand retains its own distinctive flavour and character. Brooke Bond is the only tea company that has its own plantations so the company expertise is based on a deep understanding of the tea plant itself: growing preparation and blending - the whole process from bush to cup. A complete manufacturing operation is performed in Manchester from receiving the goods raw in chests and bags to packing them into finished articles ready for the shops.

In the 1980s the series departed briefly from the 'slice of life' approach with the launch of the spy-thriller spoof starring 'Bond...Brooke Bond'. That all action hero is briefed by the British Secret Tea Service to safeguard the secret of PG Tips. Those adverts see 'Bond' skating over frozen lakes and leaping barriers as well as sauntering down the platform at 'Instant-bul' to board the Leyton Orient Express.

The decade of the 1980s saw the celebration of 25 years of the PG Chimps TV commercials. The anniversary was celebrated in style in January 1982 with a party attended by Brooke Bond, Cyril the Cyclist, scriptwriter Tony Toller, voice-over stars such as Irene Handle, Pat Coombs, Keith Connor and John Junkin as well as an ITN film crew and over 40 reporters.

The 1990s saw the return of the 'slice of life' series with the saga of the Tipps family, Geoff, Shirley, Kevin and Samantha. In 1996 the PG Chimps celebrated 40 years in the advertising business. Commemorative merchandise included calendars, tea card and cuddly toy chimps.

Over the years successful merchandising spin-offs including tea towels, painting books, stationery, toy cars and soft toys. Many of us will have owned at least one of these items. Probably the most famous promotional items however are the Sergeant Chimp Money Box and

Top: Staff gathered together at the Reebok Stadium.
Above and right: *Production today in Brooke Bond's hi-tech factory.*

Trafford Park is the most advanced tea manufacturing plant in Europe. Investment in new technology is key to maintaining that position in addition to keeping costs low and quality and customer service high. Most recently extensive investment has taken place to upgrade facilities and install unique machinery to produce the Pyramid tea bags. These have proved to be a huge success in national sales in the UK and in some countries in Europe.

At Trafford Park around 200 million tea bags and nearly half a million packets of loose tea are packed every week. Nationally we drink enough PG Tips every day to fill six Olympic sized swimming pools! Positive proof that Manchester's Brooke Bond cuppa remains the most popular drink in the UK. The firm has certainly come a long way since Arthur Brooke opened his small shop in Market Street back in 1869!

Banking on the past to ensure a brighter future

During the late 1800s Manchester's dependence on cotton manufacture was brought home by the Cotton famine whose origins lay in the loss of cotton production during the American Civil War. The need to find new sources of raw cotton was to eventually lead to the building of the Manchester Ship Canal. Amongst those affected by the cotton shortage was Henry Cooke who left the cotton trade and turned instead to stockbroking. In 1866 Thomas Knight, a member of the Manchester Stock Exchange, joined forces with Henry Cooke to found the firm which would become Henry Cooke & Son.

In 1866 stock exchange dealings were transacted not only on the floor of the Manchester Stock

Exchange but also in many meeting-places in the area. Nearby was Willoughby's, a long famous Manchester restaurant, as well as such unofficial but popular places as the Bodega, Sinclair's and Sam's Chop House.

It was in the heart of this area, and at the geographical centre of Manchester, at St Ann's Churchyard that the original offices of Henry Cooke & Son were situated. It was a good location and remained the home of the firm for over 90 years, apart from a brief period in King Street during the rebuilding of the St Ann's Churchyard premises.

Financial ability ran in the Cooke family for Henry's brother, Thomas, became Chairman of the Board of Directors of the Manchester and Liverpool District Bank. During these years railways reached their peak of importance, and ironworks attracted an accelerated flow of capital from 1865 to 1874, then declined in value over the following decade.

Above: *Henry Cooke, founder of the firm.*
Below: *Manchester Stock Exchange in the late 19th century.*

In 1898 Henry Cooke & Son handled the first issue of debenture stock on behalf of John Summers & Sons Ltd. Investments in gas undertakings grew strongly between 1865 and 1874 and more so still in the next decade. Investment abroad increased more than three fold between 1865 and 1885. With investment growing on this scale Henry Cooke was joined by his son H. Reginald Cooke in 1884.

Throughout this period and later, the trend in the Lancashire cotton industry was away from small family businesses and towards public companies. The leading companies had thousands of shareholders and there was a correspondingly large number of daily transactions in these shares.

All these widening opportunities for investment were accompanied by a growing complexity in the nature of the firm's business. There was a new awareness of the importance of rapid means of communication and more efficient types of office equipment. New tools to do the job such as the telephone and the

typewriter were introduced. The firm continued to grow so that by 1891 a total of 20 staff were able to join in celebrating the firm's silver jubilee.

In 1892 John Hunter and John Swale became partners in the firm. The name Hunter recurs many times in the history of the firm. John Hunter recognised the importance of Manchester as an investment centre as opportunities for investment continued to grow, becoming ever more diverse, reflecting an increasing variety of industry in the area.

Domestic capital investment, which had risen to a peak of about eight per cent in the 1870s, fell to perhaps less than six per cent between 1885 and 1894 and then rose again at the turn of the century, particularly in foreign investments before the first world war.

This was the situation when the second member of the Hunter family, the younger John Hunter, joined the firm becoming a partner in 1907. In 1913 when H. Reginald Cooke retired the two remaining partners were members of the Hunter family - and more were to follow.

The decade following the first world war brought a new spirit of investment in which Henry Cooke & Son participated. By 1922, when David Frank Hunter (brother of the younger John Hunter) and John Tarbett became partners, Manchester was second only to London in the volume and variety of dealings in industrial shares. The immediate reason was the short-lived post war boom in the Lancashire cotton industry which had wide effects on investment in such fields as textile machinery, chemicals and dyes. The development of the artificial silk industry also opened up new fields for investment. Shares in engineering firms in the Manchester area and elsewhere had grown in importance as had iron, steel and colliery transactions. From the end of the war to 1926 the number of miscellaneous industrial issues increased about four fold.

Above: *An early telephone directory.*
Top: *St Ann's Churchyard.*

The new trend in investment was to spread capital over an increasingly wide range of growing industries including electricity supply, gas and electrical appliances, gramophone makers, tobacco, soap, wallpaper, asbestos, catering, brewing and communications.

Bank and insurance shares offered particular rewards during this period as a result of several amalgamations.

With gradual restoration of confidence after the Wall Street Crash increasing amounts of capital were invested in dollar securities during the mid 1930s. Henry Cooke & Son adapted themselves to these changing needs and by 1939, on the outbreak of the second world war, staff numbered 34.

Six years later at the close of hostilities the immediate post war period produced special problems of its own in the form of Foreign Exchange Control, strict control of the new issue market, the abnormally low interest rates, the re-equipping of industry and nationalisation.

Despite these problems the firm prospered. The re-establishment of Germany and Japan and the scheme for the resumption of their foreign debt services, the Companies Act 1948, the continuing re-equipping of industry, the gradual relaxation of war time controls and the development of new industries and new techniques provided a steadily widening field for investment.

Gradually these new fields for investment produced a new type of investor and a wider awareness and acceptance of share ownership attracted a considerably increased number of investors.

The Stock Exchange, traditionally suspicious of publicity, now opened its gallery to the public. Henry Cooke & Son found new ways of advising investors of new opportunities. New and swifter methods of communication were introduced.

Above: John Summers & Sons Ltd's first debenture stock issue. Below: The firm's centenary dinner held on Saturday 19th November 1966.

More importantly new men with the specialised qualifications which were now needed joined the firm. In 1953 David Hunter, son of the younger John Hunter, joined the firm followed by five other new partners over the next eight years.

In 1955 Charles Colebourn became a partner, having started as personal assistant to the younger John Hunter.

A year later Gilbert Sheldon, one of the firm's representatives on the floor of the Manchester Stock Exchange, joined the partnership.

Geoffrey Furness, an economist and statistician, who played a lead part in developing the firm's investment research department, and Brian Williams, a barrister, became partners in 1959 and David Pitt, whose background was insurance broking, joined the firm in 1961.

At the end of 1965 two further additions to the partnership were Alan Ferguson and Michael Brown. The former had then had eight years experience of the investment business before joining the firm whilst the latter had previously been engaged in economic research before becoming head of Henry Cooke's Research Department. A later partner was Brian Bibby, who was a retired navy commander, in charge of office administration.

Above: *Arkwright House.*

Not only were personnel changing with the passing years. By 1957 the firm had outgrown its offices in St Ann's Churchyard and moved to larger premises in Old Colony House. And by 1966 the firm was being run from Arkwright House, Parsonage Gardens in Manchester.

In addition to the establishment of various specialist departments, expert staff had been introduced to provide periodical examination of investment portfolios and to make personal visits to clients. Increasing stress too was being placed in the mid 1960s on visits to industrial companies to obtain a comprehensive assessment of their potential for investment. In its centenary year in 1966 the firm could look at its surroundings and see itself at the heart of a vast industrial and commercial complex which attracted business from all over the country. That included that of the institutions with their powerful resources previously largely confined to the square mile of the City of London. By 1966 institutional business was greater than ever before while trustee investment, formerly limited to government and other gilt edge securities, could include many equity shares with a consequent increase in the volume and variety of investment.

Post war development had seen increasing calls for advice and assistance on all forms of public issues. Henry Cooke & Son were equipped to advise private companies on the desirability of going public and of the relative merits of the various ways of doing so.

Such assistance was of course preceded by a careful and detailed examination of all aspects of the company in question.

The new scale of activity was reflected by the growth of the firm since the second world war. By 1966 staff numbers had risen to 120. A merger in 1966 with another old-established Manchester firm Coppock & Bratby helped extend the firm's range of services.

The firm remained a partnership until 1972 when it was incorporated as an unlimited company under the same name. Almost coinciding with the transfer of membership of all firms comprising The Federation of Stock Exchanges in Great Britain and Ireland to The Stock Exchange London, in 1973 Henry Cooke & Son merged with Lumsden & Co. This London firm had acted as one of Henry Cooke's agents in the London market for some 70 years. So it was that Henry Cooke, Lumsden & Co (HCL) came to be established, with offices in Manchester and London, registering as a limited company - Henry Cooke, Lumsden Limited - in 1984 and as a plc in 1987.

In April 1980 the principals of another firm of brokers, Burge & Co, joined the London office as associates. One of those principals had practised in Llandudno, North Wales and continued to do so until 1986 when he formed the North Wales branch office of the firm.

The new firm grew rapidly in the 1980s largely as a result of being appointed as regional co-ordinator for most of the privatisation share issues.

Below: *Ledgers and Contracts Dept, Arkwright House in the 1960s.* **Bottom:** *The Centenary Dinner.*

In 1986 HCL sponsored the formation of Edington plc to provide a fully integrated range of financial and banking services for medium sized companies and high net worth individuals; Edington's business was primarily located in the north of England. In September 1988, by way of a scheme of arrangement, HCL merged with Edington to form the Henry Cooke Group plc.

In January 1989 the business of Howitt & Pemberton was acquired to establish a branch office for HCL and Henry Cooke Corporate Finance in Leeds.

In April 1991 difficulties were experienced by several smaller banking businesses in the UK and Edington applied for voluntary Administration. This significantly reduced the group's net assets. That unhappy event caused a mercifully short-lived loss of client confidence: subsequently the position was recovered and depositors eventually received a return on their money amounting to 105p in the pound.

David Hunter (whose grandfather John Hunter joined Henry Cooke 30 years after the firm's formation) and the last member of the Hunter family to work in the group retired in 1993, having been chairman for over 30 years. Many changes lay ahead.

In December 1994 a team from Seymour Pierce Butterfield joined the London office shortly before

Above: The office in the late 1950s. **Right:** David Hunter, who retired in 1993.

it moved to new premises at Piercy House. In May 1995 a new management team was appointed who have changed the emphasis of the business from stockbroking to investment management and improved the profitability of the group. In January 1996, as part of this change, the group out-sourced its settlement and client custody facilities to Pershing Securities Ltd.

In March 1999, the Henry Cooke Group was acquired by Brown, Shipley & Co Ltd, a merchant and private bank based in London, which is itself wholly owned by Kredietbank Luxembourg. As a result, the firm has now added a range of banking services to its established areas of business: private client investment management, collective fund management, charity and pension fund management and corporate broking services. From its recently refurbished premises in King Street the business manages funds of over one billion pounds, a reflection of the enormous wealth which the business has helped Manchester accumulate since the days of Queen Victoria.

A catalogue of triumph

Long before the Internet and the World Wide Web arrived in our lives the initials WWW were already familiar to the people of Manchester; the intitials standing for World-wide Wholesale Warehouses - an integral part of the huge mail order business of J D Williams & Co Ltd.

The story behind today's J D Williams mail order company is a complex one and draws several strands of business history together.

One strand began in 1859 when one George Oxendale opened a drapers shop near the Black Bull Hotel in Northallerton. He quickly gained a reputation for value and service and his business flourished.

Sixteen years later in 1875 nineteen year old James David Williams was living in Derby - and he was in trouble. After some years working in the clothing trade and with a capital of just £13 10s he had decided to work for himself. Promised good sales from a clothing club operated by the Butterley Mining Company for its employees young James had purchased a great deal of stock; sadly he soon discovered that his 'customers' had bought elsewhere or paid old bills instead.

Recalling those events fifty years later J D Williams recounted 'I was completely done, but I borrowed an old two-wheeled cart and put in all my stock and drove to Brackwell, a colliery village near Alpeton, and sold the goods from the cart cash down. I was able in this way to utilise the stock and found I could easily take £10-15 per day and make more money'.

Above: *James David (J D) Williams, who established his business in 1875.*
Below and facing page top: *The offices which indicate the size of the operation even in the 1930s.*

From that uncertain start James Williams managed to expand; he was soon running three specially built mobile shops which opened at the back to form a counter and doors at the sides opening in the middle, one portion forming a counter and the other half a roof. Soon however J D found that what he called the 'Letter Order' part of his trade was growing.

In February 1881 James gave up personally running his van trade and took premises in St Mary's Gate in Derby from which to run his fledgling mail order business.

The times were perfect and J D had stumbled on a gold mine, although it took him some years to realise it.

Above: *An early promise to 'Please our customers' which was posted in every department.*

For the first time in history a truly successful mail order business could be operated on a large scale as a result of events far beyond J D Williams control. The reasons were two fold: most significantly because of the Compulsory Education Act of 1870 for the first time nearly everyone over the age of fifteen could read and write and could thus use a catalogue to buy goods.

The second fortuitous event arrived on 1 August 1882 when the Post Office launched the Parcel Post a much cheaper delivery service than that previously offered by the railways. James Williams was there at 7 am on that first day with his Letter Order parcels at Derby General Post Office.

Derby however was not really the best place to be. Within a short space of time James had realised that Manchester was THE business centre of the day, so in 1884 he moved to premises in Manchester's Watling Street - trading as J D Williams & Co, although in fact there were no partners in the firm. Over the next four years the business expanded, in 1888 buying out Manchester's Dress Manufacturing Company, the first of many other business acquisitions, and moving to premises at 34 Charlotte Street. In 1885 land was bought in Princess Street to build a warehouse, premises which almost never opened due to a disastrous fire which broke out in the building just before completion in 1907 - fortunately by that time the firm also had a second warehouse in Dale Street.

By 1896 however, long before the great Princess Street fire J D Williams felt able to write 'For the first time I felt I was getting on my feet'.

At about that time George Oxendale of Northallerton died and his business passed to his keen grandson Frank Fairbank who promptly instigated the well-overdue expansion of his conservative grandfather's premises.

By 1902 Oxendale's had grown and so had its mail order business. A section of the newly-extended premises had to be given over to dealing solely with orders received by post. Then Oxendale's first advert appeared in the press.

very elegant building - Granby House - in Granby Row Manchester.

At the same time J D Williams and his grown up sons were forced to find larger premises. Building continued at the ideally located site in Dale Street. Still business grew even faster.

Above: *The offices in the early 1930s.*
Below: *The directors, families and committee - Diamond Jubilee presentation, April 8th, 1935.*

It was a bold step. Frank Fairbank searched the markets, bought favourably and hoped.

The stock sold out. People talked of the bargains they had received; then there were more adverts and then a catalogue. Oxendale's prospered, but as the business grew so did the problems of transport and warehouse capacity, delivery deadlines and associated expenses.

In 1907 Oxendale's took the boldest step in the firm's history and built a

While those two companies were busily expanding a Londoner, Frank Derry, was facing ruin. The most recent of his many business ventures had failed, and if it had not been for his season ticket he would not even have been able to travel home to Woking!

But on that journey home he had a good idea. Needing capital he offered to live in a well-known haunted house. The owner, a doctor could neither sell nor let the house because of its terrible reputation; he offered Frank a year's rent free tenancy, and £50, if the Derry family lived in the house for a year to break the alleged curse.

With the money Frank could put an idea into action; he devised a webbing belt for men fitted with four magnets and sold it with the suggestion that it would enhance the wearer's health and increase their 'masculine vigour' - a delicate euphemism of the times.

The 'Magnet' belt was perfectly suited to its day and age and so when offered by post at five shillings (25p) 'Yours for one shilling deposit and four one shilling payments weekly' it was an overnight success.

The first response to Frank's advert was received on 22 March 1911. Demand grew and there were more and more requests for a larger surgical belt with the same alleged magnetic benefits. So Frank Derry introduced his 'Hercules' belt priced at two guineas (£2.10) and also offered on easy terms. But still-wider horizons beckoned - only a small percentage of men wore a belt, but nearly every woman wore a corset!

So the Magnet Corset was launched, a fine support garment with magnetised metal stays. Press advertising backed up by a diligent Repeat Ordering Department specialising in intensive customer cultivation maintained a buoyant market and ultimately Ambrose Wilson, the business founded by Frank Derry, became the largest mail order corset house in the world.

J D Williams & Co became a private limited company in December 1921. The founder's four sons; Ernest, Perceval, George and Leonard had been in the family business since before 1907 and were now given equal capital and shares to carry on the business. 'The Governor' as J D was always fondly remembered had eventually been overwhelmed by his own success and by the 1920s, according to his son George, the business had grown far beyond his father's capacity to control its workings. The Governor died in 1925. By the time of the founder's death the business he had started had grown from having annual sales in 1895 of £7,357 to a business with a yearly turnover of more than half a million pounds.

And the rest is history: even in the terrible years of recession and depression during the 1920s and 30s only in one year, 1928, did the firm's sales briefly drop. In 1933, for the first time, the firm actually received over one million orders from customers in a single year.

In October 1963 the issued share capital was bought from the Williams family by Cooper-Taymil Limited a subsidiary of Alliance Brothers Limited led by David (later Sir David) Alliance and his brother Nigel.

Above: *Early examples of the catalogues issued.*

In March 1970 agreement was reached with David Alliance, the controlling shareholder, with the board of Northern Counties Securities Ltd - Oxendale's parent company - for its acquisition by N Brown Investments. The J D Williams share capital was transferred to N Brown for £1,400,000. The Alliance share capital was sold off to the textile company Spirella leaving the Brown Group with Ambrose Wilson, J A Davis (which had been acquired in July 1969) and J D Williams all three of which were involved in the mail order business.

After a shaky financial start the companies began to expand at an extraordinary rate, each of the three businesses complementing one another.

Shortly afterwards 'Dale House' was created from the acquisition of two mail order companies, Quality Post from the Burton Group and Halwins. Their ranges of merchandise were consolidated although both titles were retained.

In the 1980s Oxendale's expanded its business into the Republic of Ireland based in Dublin. Aldrex, a small company based in Newham, Gloucester, was bought in 1987; its customer profile was very similar to Ambrose Wilson in catering for the slightly older woman. Bury Boot and Shoe Company and Whitfords mail order companies had been in existence since just after the second world war. Mr Whitford died in the 1980s and both businesses were acquired by J D Williams; their clients were very similar and today those two companies, together with Aldrex, operate from a base in Bury.

Heather Valley was originally a mail order bespoke tailoring business based in Edinburgh. Country Garden , formerly an independent company selling up market gardening products, was bought in 1986. And in 1987 the Hartingdon House business was acquired. The customers of all three catalogues were in similar socio-economic groups so J D Williams decided to concentrate its strategy and create one catalogue for all three ranges of merchandise.

Above: *One of the machines which printed the catalogues. At the time it was the largest of its kind in the world.*
Below and facing page top: *The Scottish Royal Show, Edinburgh in 1948.*

The J D Williams Group had been acquired by N Brown Investments, also owned by David Alliance, in a reverse take-over designed to secure a public quotation on the stock market. In 1986 the company name was changed to N Brown Group plc.

In 1989 J D Williams launched two new titles to further expand its customer profile - the Special Collection and Candid.

Alongside Candid the firm also launched Fashion World: the two new catalogues were a deliberate attempt to introduce the company to a younger market aged between 25 and 40. The company had noted that many women who are over size 16 had difficulty finding clothes at the right size and right price in the high street. Fashion World aimed to provide fashionable, affordable clothes in a wide range of sizes to women whose needs did not meet the fashion industry's usual templates.

Five years later, in 1994, J D Williams launched yet another range of women's clothes, the Classic Combination intended to provide women aged 30 to 45 with better fitting clothes, a need which had been identified by a national size survey. The aim was to re-cut patterns to fit the woman of the nineties, not women of the fifties on whom many standard clothing industry patterns were still based. Most recently, in April 1999

Above right: *J D Williams' premises today.*
Right: *J D Williams' Spring 2000 catalogue.*

the firm's Simply Be range of clothing was launched. That newest range of clothing is aimed at aspirational women under the age of 40. Young, stylish, fashionable clothing in sizes 16-30 now offers customers a degree of choice that they may have never previously experienced.

By following the founder's original standards of service and value J D Williams enjoys an unrivalled position in today's market place despite increasing competition, adverse trading conditions and ever more complex legislation.

Today J D Williams forms the largest part of the N Brown group of companies with its headquarters at 53 Dale Street Manchester. It is now a top 200 company on the stock exchange. Annual turnover exceeds three hundred million pounds and pre-tax profits exceed forty millions annually

Five generations of the Williams family were eventually to work for the company which bears their name - and the family still has one director on the board; today however the Alliance family are the major shareholders.

In keeping with its founder's endless search for business opportunities the firm has now taken advantage of the latest development in retailing - the Internet. J D Williams has now developed a forwarding service for Internet sales companies allowing them to utilise J D Williams' vast home delivery network. A fine example of one WWW meeting the needs of another WWW!

A loch of lager in Moss Side

Scottish Courage's Royal Brewery in Moss Side's Denmark Road is a familiar sight to the residents of Manchester on their way to the City using the Princess Parkway. Many may recall that local landmark, the brewery's red brick tower, which stood on Denmark Road for nearly a century before it vanished in the late 1970s, under the enormous expansion for the modern lager brewery.

Originally the Albert Brewery, and later renamed simply the Moss Side Brewery, it was built around 1875 and named after Queen Victoria's late husband Prince Albert.

Brewing began under William Brookes, the first of many owners, who had begun brewing at least ten years earlier. He had occupied the Eclipse Brewery on Lad Lane Deansgate and run the nearby Eclipse Vaults before he moved, first to the Hulme Brewery in City Road and then to Moss Side.

Helped by his son George, William Brookes employed about two dozen men and kept eight horses for deliveries.

The water used by the Brewery was noted for its exceptional quality: according to one contemporary source 'containing all the necessary elements for producing the finest ales which cannot be surpassed in the district for their brightness, purity and flavour'.

The Brookes supplied ales and stouts to several local tied beer houses such as the Shah Inn on Hargreaves Street in Hulme and the Cross Keys in Salford; they also supplied a far larger number of free houses. On the death of William Brookes his trustees sold the Albert Brewery to John Henry Lees.

John Henry Lees can be traced back to 1848 when the firm of James and William Lees founded the Town Lane Brewery in Denton - a surprisingly substantial enterprise which included such modern sounding facilities as laboratories and a refrigeration plant.

John Henry Lees arrived at the Albert Brewery in 1894 and shortly afterwards changed the name to the Moss Side Brewery; he was soon able to expand the business and his company, J H Lees Ltd, controlled 23 pubs. Under his ownership the prefix 'Royal' was added to the name in honour of King Edward VII's visit to Manchester in 1907.

By 1910 John Lees was in ill health and without his hand at the tiller the business fell into financial difficulties. In January 1913 an official receiver was appointed and, with no pun intended, John Henry Lees Ltd went into liquidation. Again ownership and production changed.

Below: *A corner of the export department dating from the 1940s with 'Red Tower lager'.*

That supposedly modern drink, lager, was first brewed at the Royal Brewery as long ago as 1927 by the Palatine Bottling Co Ltd, a subsidiary company of a very large local brewery firm of the time, Walker & Homfrays Ltd, which had absorbed the Royal Moss Side Brewery and its by then 19 pubs in 1922. Another name change was the order of the day and The Red Tower Lager Brewery Ltd was incorporated in 1933. The Company named its lager 'Red Tower' associating the name with the main architectural feature of the building. The name 'Royal Brewery' however appears to have been retained as an address.

In the early 1930s a new brewing plant capable of producing 100 barrels in one mash was installed. In 1935 new conical fermenters were added which were the first ever in the UK and they are still in use today.

Red Tower lager was launched onto the London market where it was mainly sold in expensive restaurants being dispensed from elegant wooden cabinets which were wheeled from table to table.

During the second world war when many restaurants in London closed down, sales of lager declined but the arrival of American troops in the Manchester area created a new local demand. Indicative of those turbulent days, the Head Brewer at that time was Anthony Musayryk, a cousin of the deposed President of Czechoslovakia.

In 1955 the Royal Moss Side Brewery Ltd was formed as a wholly owned subsidiary of the Red Tower Lager Brewery Ltd, just prior to its acquisition by Scottish Brewers. They bought the Brewery as a means of expansion south and also to produce their own McEwan Younger (MY) Lager.

When Scottish & Newcastle Breweries, Guinness and Courage later formed a consortium to produce and market Harp Lager the Royal Brewery was chosen as one of the production sites; brewing of Harp commenced in 1962.

During the following four years the amazing growth in demand for lager led to the decision that a major expansion of the Brewery was necessary.

It was during this period that the existing Brewhouse and the huge skyscraper maturation block which now dominates the site replaced the old red tower as the Brewery's landmark. Until 1979 the Royal Brewery was a single-product site. In 1979 however the Harp consortium was disbanded with Scottish and Newcastle retaining ownership of the Royal Brewery.

Above: Denmark Road in 1970 with new vessels arriving.

McEwans Lager which had been introduced to the market in 1978 started being
brewed at the Royal Brewery in 1980.

Until 1985 all beer produced was sent off
site in 120 barrel tankers to be put in
kegs at other S&N breweries or sent to
other companies to package on their
sites such as Greene King,
Wolverhampton and Dudley and
Burtonwood.

S&N now decided to develop further the
Royal Brewery and set up a planning
partnership with the City Council, which
involved a land swap and the closure of
Denmark Road. In addition the Council
wanted to improve the quality of
housing in Moss Side and Hulme as well
as increasing employment so
substandard housing was cleared to
create the space required for the
expansion.

A sum of £8 million was spent on building
the resultant Bulk Packaging plant which enables the
site to package 11 and 22 gallon containers - the first
kegs came off the line in May 1986.

Above: Bottom of the fermentation vessells in the 1970s.
Below: Denmark Road and the 'Red Tower' Brewery in the 1960s.

This put packaging facilities back on the Royal site for the first time in 30 years. This was quickly followed in 1990 by a new Canning plant, allowing the site to supply the ever growing off licence and supermarket trade which now accounts for half of the product from the site.

In 1995 Scottish and Newcastle PLC acquired Courage Ltd's brewing business forming Scottish Courage Brewing - the UK's largest brewer.

From an output of two million hls in 1996 Royal Brewery currently has an output of over three million. A level of production helped no doubt by the introduction of the enormously successful Foster's Lager which now accounts for 75 per cent of output. In total, this means the site now produces a staggering 13 million pints a week.

The Brewery also produces many other familiar brand names - Kronenbourg 1664, Miller Pils, McEwans Lager, Kestrel and Hofmeister. Two hundred and thirty five employees work on the site with many recruited locally during the packaging expansion.

Over 125 years and from humble beginnings, through continuous change and development, the Royal Brewery has secured not only its survival but its prosperity. Its huge production represents about six per cent of all beer consumed in the UK, and is the largest Brewery in Manchester or indeed the North West of England.

All of this amazing increase in size and efficiency of the Brewery has not been at the cost of outstanding quality though. Indeed, in the Year 2000, Foster's Lager from the Brewery was awarded the Gold Medal at the International Brewing Awards, the 'Oscars' of the brewing industry. This competition, which had a total of 700 entries and was judged by 'blind' tasting by Brewers from around the world, has clearly demonstrated that the beers from Royal remain 'unsurpassed in the district for their brightness, purity and flavour'.

Were the ghost of William Brookes to return to the site of his original brewery there might be little today that he would recognise - but there is no doubt that he would instantly identify with the product and cheerfully raise a glass to the continuing success of the brewing business!

Top right: *The Royal Brewery today.* ***Top left:*** *Tom Ward, Managing Director, Scottish Courage Brewing, awarding Nigel Rutherford, Brewing Manager, the Gold Medal for Foster's Lager.* ***Left:*** *Foster's Lager coming off the line at 3,000 cans per minute.*

Putting the 'star' in starch

Whether you are aware of it or not, it is probable that everyone reading this book will have at some time or other experienced the produce of Trafford Park's Cerestar company. And yet few of us will have linked the huge site next to the Ship Canal with our everyday lives.

The Manchester mill and glucose refinery of Cerestar UK is one of the largest in Europe. Each day more than 1,000 tonnes of maize are processed there to extract starch, protein, germ and fibre. Starch is itself then used as the feed stock for the production of glucose syrups and dextrose monohydrate as well as simply being dried to produce cornflour. The protein and fibre are dried for use in animal feed whilst the germ goes for further processing to extract the maize oil. This oil, after refining, appears on the supermarket shelves as maize cooking oil.

Today Cerestar is part of the Eridania Béghin-Say group of companies, one of the most important agro-industrial businesses in the world with its headquarters in Paris. But how did this massive plant whose products are extensively used in food, confectionery, brewing, pharmaceuticals, paper and many other products begin?

The name Cerestar appeared only in 1987 when the US parent company sold its European Corn Wet Milling business which included Trafford Park's CPC UK Ltd. In the resulting change of ownership the firm of Cerestar UK Ltd came into being, inheriting CPC's mantle. The central business of milling and refining however has roots which go back a very long way indeed.

The word starch itself indicates its long usage, stemming as it does from the Anglo-Saxon word 'stearc' meaning 'that which is or makes strong' a clear reference to its early use in laundry work.

Certainly starch was in common in use the monasteries of medieval England. By the mid 16th century records show that starch was being imported in large quantities from the Low Countries to stiffen linen and the ever more flamboyant lace ruffs of the fashionable clothing of the times. The Puritans took offence at this, as at so many fripperies, and adopted the habit using only blue starch in their clothing - a practice which was forbidden by Elizabeth the First in 1596 under penalty of imprisonment!

Starch can be and was produced from a variety of vegetable substances: potatoes, rice and sago for example as well as from wheat and maize.

Above: *Unloading maize from a ship moored at Brown & Polson's Wharf in the early 1960s.* ***Below:*** *The Nicholl's Nagel & Co. plant viewed from the north side of the Ship Canal around 1920.*

It was in the 1840s that commercial starch manufacture began in Britain by suppliers such as Reckitt, Colmans and Brown and Polson. Those companies sold their starch powder for laundry use.

Before the 1850s the best quality starch available was that extracted from rice with sago starch a close second. Brown and Polson's first venture was the manufacture and sale of their 'Powder Starch' made from sago flour in their Scottish factory.

In 1854 production of maize starch was introduced by Brown and Polson using a wet milling process invented by John Polson.

Wet milling begins with the maize undergoing a softening process by 'steeping' under carefully controlled conditions for up to 40 hours. Following this the softened grain is lightly milled to break up the kernel and release the undamaged oil-bearing maize germ. After separation the result is a slurry composed of starch, protein and fibre. Further grinding reduces the starch and protein components to a very fine particle size and the fibre can be

separated by screening. Today centrifuges separate the starch and protein. The final stage in the extraction of starch consists of a washing process which removes the remaining protein and produces a starch slurry which is then either dried or used as feed stock for glucose syrups and dextrose.

The importance of Brown and Polson's breakthrough cannot be overestimated; the milling of maize or corn had not previously been a very worthwhile proposition because of the oily 'impurities' which it contained and its relative indigestibility. Brown and Polson working in Paisley in Scotland solved the problem of milling maize without rupturing the corn germ and releasing the unwanted oil it contained. The process involved 37 different operations resulting in not only a virtually pure starch but also a separation of the other parts of the maize which could then be dried and ground to be sold as cattle feed. With cheap American maize available in almost unlimited quantities Brown and Polson's business was set to boom, not least when it was realised that food for human consumption might also be produced.

Not surprisingly by the time John Polson died in 1900 aged 75 he was a millionaire, one of the wealthiest industrialists in Britain.

In producing an oil-free cornstarch, Brown and Polson discovered that they had found an ingredient that had the potential for use in a wide range of food products. Adapting the process slightly they produced a finely ground corn starch which was patented under the name 'Brown and Polson's

*Top: An aerial view of the Corn Products Factory in the late 1920s. **Above left:** Check weighing of drums of glucose in the 1950s.*

Patent Corn Flour'. The new food could be used as a baby and invalid food and became the basis for a whole new range of blancmanges (then still the two words 'blanc mange') and custards and as the standard thickener for gravy and soup. The new product soon became known to the public simply as cornflour though to the trade it remained 'Brown and Polson's PCF'.

Corn Products Co Ltd, later known as CPC and Cerestar's immediate corporate predecessor, was formed in 1903 as the British subsidiary of the American company whose main interest was the export of starch to the UK for refining.

By 1911 the USA was exporting over 30,000 tonnes of maize starch to the UK. In that year the firm of Nicholls, Nagle and Co built the first wet milling plant and glucose refinery on the Trafford Park site. Thirteen years later, in 1924, the Corn Products Company, bought the plant and started to manufacture glucose from dry starch imported from the USA.

The Corn Products Company, or CPC, acquired Brown and Polson and its wet milling facilities in 1935 for one million pounds. By 1938 the expanding firm had captured 40 per cent of the UK glucose market, mostly produced in Manchester.

After the passage of another eighteen years, in 1955, Brown and Polson, now a wholly owned subsidiary of CPC, decided to extend the Manchester site due to its proximity to the Ship Canal. A seven hundred foot wharf, wet milling plant, starch drier, dextrose plant and new glucose refinery were added to the site.

The wharf has enabled many seagoing ships to discharge their bulk cargoes of maize directly into the company's

silos. One of the most well-known of those vessels was the *S. S. Carchester,* a purpose built grain carrier with a very shallow draught to allow navigation of the Ship Canal, and which only just fitted between the lock gates. Fully laden, the *S. S. Carchester* was able to carry 17,500 tonnes of maize from the USA.

During the 1960s production continued to increase not least when the firm switched to a three shift day, seven days per week, 340 days per year. That increase in production allowed Manchester to take over completely from Paisley as a starch producer. The oldest wet milling plant in the world was to be put to other uses as the distinction between the industrial and consumer sides of Brown and Polson was emphasised.

Above: A Brown & Polson 'black and white' tanker and employee. ***Below:*** *Open day visitors viewing the CPC engine in the 1970s.*

An indication of that change of emphasis in the firm's business came in 1971 when Brown and Polson changed its name to CPC Ltd, a blow to the people of Paisley who had perhaps long laboured under the illusion that their home-town firm had taken over CPC rather than the other way around.

In more recent times more changes have been seen on the Trafford Park site: in 1990 the company spent £60 million in a new refinery and in 1994 a new administration and laboratory complex was completed, part of the changed infrastructure around the new canal bridge. Since then further significant investments have taken place in new plant and equipment to maintain the company's position as the leading supplier of glucoses and starchy products in the UK.

Today Cerestar's site occupies 35 acres beside the Ship Canal, with output from the plant exceeding 300,000 tonnes per annum of finished product. To produce this output the company generates its own power and

steam from a gas turbine CHP plant which is used to generate 10-12 megawatts of electricity each hour. Much of the production today leaves the plant in bulk road tankers and rail wagons, with deliveries being made to customers the length and breadth of the UK.

The next time you read the ingredients on a packet of food and see in the list the words glucose syrup or maize starch, or pick up a piece of corrugated cardboard and perhaps briefly wonder what kind of adhesive is used in its manufacture then spare a moment to think of Trafford Park and Cerestar. The chances are that, thanks to the 19th century ingenuity of John Polson, the product had its origins on the banks of the Manchester Ship Canal.

Top: *Part of the 1970s fleet.* **Right and above left:** *The Trafford Park premises today.*

Dunlop GRG - still not tyred of the rain

Lancashire is famous for its rain, perhaps it was no coincidence then the city of Manchester became the first place in the world to manufacture water proof clothing! For three generations the name of Dunlop and its GRG (general rubber goods) division has been indelibly linked with rubber and rubber products in the city.

Dunlop has however been involved in Manchester only since 1925 when it acquired the Cambridge Street premises of Macintosh & Co. The history of rubber in Manchester goes back much further than that.

It was in 1820 in Glasgow that Charles Macintosh discovered that coal tar naphtha was an effective solvent for rubber - and in London that Thomas Hancock invented the rubber 'masticator' a critical element in making the industrial use of rubber practical.

Before vulcanisation was discovered, heating rubber in order to stabilise it, rubber was a sticky substance thought to be of little use. Macintosh's genius lay in his 1823 patent in which he demonstrated his idea of creating a double texture waterproof fabric with a tacky rubber solution sandwiched between the two layers of 'rain proof' cloth. This was the first application of rubber to command a mass market - and it made Macintosh's name a household word synonymous with the rain coat.

Four years later Macintosh began his long association with Manchester when he joined forces with Birley's

cotton manufacturers to form Charles Macintosh and Co. The new firm became the owner of the Chorlton Old Mill on the banks of the now culverted River Medlock ten minutes walk from Manchester's City Hall. Under the partnership arrangements Charles Macintosh received five- seventeenths of the firm's profits with the remainder split between the Manchester firms of Birley & Kirk, and H T & R Barton. The rubber-naphtha solution was made in Glasgow in the secret recesses of Macintosh's high-walled Dunchattan works and sent to Manchester by canal. The new water proof Macintosh cloth was sold as piece goods to be cut into cloaks and capes by clothing manufacturers elsewhere.

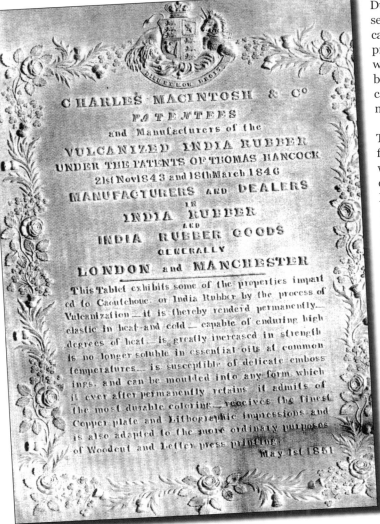

The early days of the fledgling rubber industry were curiously close ones: in 1833 Macintosh's niece had married a Monsieur Daubree who eventually started the firm which would in due course become Michelin: no-one would have guessed at the time what such a development would eventually lead to. The following year Hancock, inventor of the masticator, joined the board of Macintosh's, an appointment which paid off handsomely when in 1843 Hancock, who had discovered vulcanisation almost simultaneously with Goodyear in the USA, patented all forms of heat curing.

Rubber was an up and coming material and rubber goods of all kinds were soon in demand, not just for Macintosh coats: perhaps one of its most curious uses

Above: *A tablet produced by Charles Macintosh from vulcanised india rubber to indicate some of its elastic properties.*

however not an auspicious period for any business - in 1929 rumours swept Manchester that the massive Cambridge Street works were to close.

Fortunately those rumours were unfounded and although the Macintosh companies were liquidated in 1933 the Dunlop group, especially its Manchester acquisitions, survived the economic storm with the whole group's rubber spreading departments being moved to Manchester.

By contrast with Macintosh's Dunlop could almost be described as a brash young upstart, Dunlop's history going back merely to 1888. It was in that year that John Boyd Dunlop a Scottish vet, then practising in Ireland, invented the first practical pneumatic tyre. The wheel, rigid since pre-historic times, could now be cushioned. The Pneumatic Tyre and Booth Cycle Agency was formed a year later to develop Dunlop's invention. His tyres were made from material bought from existing rubber firms but within a few years the company had bought its own manufacturers, Byrne Brothers of Birmingham.

Dunlop's pneumatic tyres quickly captured the imagination of the world. Demand was so high that by the turn of the century the company had set up manufacturing and sales companies in Australia, Canada, France, Germany and South Africa.

being when in 1904 the courtyard of the Savoy Hotel in London was paved with Macintosh rubber slabs at a cost of what was then considered the extraordinary sum of £2,000.

In 1925 Macintosh & Co was acquired by Dunlop the new industrial group including amongst its many parts the Manchester Balata Belting Company. The 1920s was

Above: *Dunlop's premises on Cambridge Street, Cholton-on-Medlock.* ***Above left:*** *Chorlton New Mill (built in 1813).*

Meanwhile in Britain, in 1900, a second factory was established in Birmingham, already the heart of the bicycle industry and the fledgling motor industry. It was in Birmingham that the company manufactured its first car tyres. That year the firm also changed its name to the Dunlop Rubber Company Ltd, a name which would remain until 1967 when the business changed its name simply to the Dunlop Company Ltd.

Having established itself as a supplier to the rapidly developing motor car industry the company was quick to realise that wheels and tyres might be thought of as a single unit and in 1906 it acquired a wheel manufacturing company in Coventry.

Attention was next directed to getting better control over Dunlop's chief raw materials, rubber and textiles. To secure the supply of rubber Dunlop began investing in Malayan estates in 1909. By the 1920s Dunlop was the single largest plantation owner in Malaya. The company achieved further control over its raw materials with the establishment of cotton mills for the supply of tyre cord and other fabrics. The first of those Dunlop mills was opened in 1916 in Rochdale. Interestingly vertical integration in this period did not extend to production of raw cotton which continued to be bought on the open market until rayon, nylon and polyester fabrics began to dominated the tyre manufacture sector. Factories were opened in Japan in 1909 and the USA in 1920. During those opening decades

of the 20th century new products were continually being developed -the famous Dunlop golf ball making its first appearance in 1908 and two years later the first Dunlop aircraft tyres.

> *With the invention of the pneumatic tyre, the previously rigid wheel could now be cushioned*

Dunlop's 1925 purchase of the Charles Macintosh group of companies was a dynamic aggressive response to the slump in world trade which followed the end of the first world war. At that time the Manchester factory was making tyres, footwear, cables, clothing and a general range of rubber goods. Dunlop quickly disposed of the cable and clothing interests but the remainder of the business provided new focus for Dunlop. The future looked good.

Alas the future cannot be predicted. In 1940 the Old Mill the original Macintosh factory was destroyed by bombing with the Cambridge Street site continuing production. During the second world war as result of the loss of Old Mill additional premises were used in City Hall, Trafford Park and Middleton, During the war the firm's production included such valuable items as barrage balloons, aero tyres, gas masks, ground sheets, inflatables, special clothing and aircraft dinghies.

The over-running of the company's Malayan rubber estates by the Japanese was serious news for the company whilst it provided an incentive to develop the firm's expertise in

Below: A meeting of over 70 ex-Dunlop staff in 1964.

making and using artificial rubber substitutes - an expertise which would pay enormous dividends in the post-war years.

The Cambridge Street factory was originally built in 1824 with various additions up to 1930; by 1970 over two thousand personnel were employed there. Corrosion resistant chemical pipe lines, marine equipment, extrusions, proofing, rubber gloves, hot water bottles, car mats, solid tyres and hydroelastic compounds are amongst the many products which have been manufactured there.

In 1982 there was a major investment at the Cambridge Street site when a fully automated computer controlled compound mixing plant was commissioned. This was at the time one of the most modern mixing facilities in Europe, and as well as producing high quality rubber compounds, substantially improved the environment by incorporating enclosed carbon black handling, with highly efficient dust extraction systems.

In 1985, the Dunlop Empire was broken up with Tyre operations being taken over by Sumitomo and the other Dunlop businesses including Dunlop GRG becoming part of BTR.

For the next twelve years Dunlop GRG continued to manufacture its wide range of products and rationalise its sites, life raft manufacture at the

Top: A Banbury internal mixer in the old mill in the 1970s. Above centre: The cover of the Dunlop Newsreel issued in November 1964.

Hindley Green factory was transferred to Beaufort in Birkenhead. The Wrexham factory and then Skelmersdale all closed, leaving the Cambridge site, which was the oldest, as the last remaining site of the old GRG division.

In 1997 Dunlop GRG, as part of the BTR 'polymer products' group was part of a management buyout of the group from BTR and a new company, UniPoly, was formed. Around this time the Cambridge Street factory began a close association with Greengate Polymer Coatings factory in Salford and in February 1999 a Buy-in-Management buy-out bought Dunlop GRG and Greengate Polymer Coatings, forming the present company, Dunlop GRG Holdings Limited.

Today Dunlop GRG Holdings is based over three sites. The Mill compound and Extrusions businesses are maintained at the Cambridge Street site, producing custom rubber compounds and rubber based extruded products for use throughout an almost infinite range of products.

At the Greengate Site a polymer coatings business produces materials used for life raft canopies, protective clothing and coated textiles for oil and water tanks, sewer refurbishment, balloon materials, and lightweight leisure wear. An Automotive flooring business manufactures high quality acoustic floor matting for commercial vehicles.

Further afield in Middleton, the flexible Fabrications business produces collapsible fuel and water tanks, towable storage barges, low pressure pneumatic fenders for the Navy, Gasometer seals and a range of equipment for the containment of oil spills.

The new Dunlop GRG company is rekindling the dynamism and innovation of the original entrepreneurs of the rubber industry. New products are actively being developed as this uniquely vertically integrated business has returned to the concepts of its founders in offering 'Engineering solutions in Rubber' across a wide range of markets.

Quite what either Charles Macintosh or John Dunlop would have made of the innovative, dynamic company their legacy has become one can only imagine. Perhaps today few spare much thought for those two pioneers - but if nothing else Mancunians cycling in the rain can thank them for being able to do so without getting sore or wet in the process!

A spark in the dark

One spark of light in the dark, gloom-laden depression years of the 1930s was the founding of the Manchester firm of A Carey & Son Ltd., Electrical Installation Engineers. The firm's founder, Albert Carey, had the benefit of sound training through a full electrical engineering apprenticeship with Ferguson and Palin Ltd. He was also growing up at a time when that most humble of electrical appliances, the domestic light bulb, was no longer quite the luxury it had once been. It was from the recognition of the benefit which his family could gain from wiring the house for electric lights which started Albert off on his own in 1932.

The conversion Albert undertook proved an excellent advertisement for the change from gas to electric - and for the standard of workmanship which he always set himself. There were neighbours who wanted similar conversions carried out and Albert gave up his job to pursue that work.

By 1936 the family business had become established with the opening of a retail outlet in Bentinck Street in Ashton-Under-Lyne. Trading in accumulators, batteries and torches never really captured Albert's imagination

however. Once the conversion work on his doorstep had dried up he spent some time hawking for work around the area on a his bicycle. Fortunately this generated contacts with local landlords and an advance in the scale of business took place with contracts to convert substantial numbers of properties for one of those landlords.

The disruption of war required Albert Carey to work on the electrics of submarines in the Vickers shipyards. This provided an insight into the problems associated with cramped working environments, difficult ventilation and air conditioning. The ingenuity with which Albert was able to overcome those problems enhanced his view of the business opportunities which arose after 1945.

The original shop, and later larger premises, still in Bentinck Street, fronted Albert's early post-war work. He did become increasingly mobile however, with first a motor bike and a side car, later three-wheeled vans and, by the mid 1950s, a Ford converted into a pick-up truck by the Lockwood and Greenwood Garage.

Above: *Carey's Investor in People certificate from 1995.* ***Below:*** *Hyde High Dependency Unit.*

For Carey Electrical Engineers the entry of Albert's son Barry into the business in 1955 was an indication of a continuity which was to develop in the training standards and practices of the firm. Barry's experience as an apprentice was no different from other recruits however. Today, as managing director, Barry still has strong memories of struggling on and off buses as an electrician's apprentice, carrying the large, heavy tool bags of more experienced men.

An illustration of Albert Carey's maturing understanding of his trade and the working practices needed to secure safe and reliable services to the community comes from his involvement with the Electrical Contractors Association; he was a founder member of the Ashton branch in the 1950s. The company has maintained an interest in the Association ever since.

What the light bulb did for Albert in the early years the computer did for Carey Electrical Engineers in the 1960s. The company took on pioneering work associated with the wiring for main-frame computers. At ease by this time in large factory sites it was possible to win large contracts for work involving power supply, hard core wiring, fire protection and air conditioning. As this side of the business expanded the shop finally had to be abandoned for larger workshop premises.

A new base was found in Guide Lane, Audenshaw where design and assembly work on control panels proved to be a natural extension of the company's business.

Much post-war reconstruction work meant house building and the supply of furniture to fill the new houses. Carey Electrical Engineering gained contracts to work in both these areas and took on apprentices as part of an early expansion programme.

In the late 1940s the firm accepted wiring contracts within the local factories which were mass producing the utility furniture of the period. Albert also worked on the wiring of new housing estates as they were developed but the firm always paid attention to the 'bread and butter' base of its work.

The most significant feature of the factory work was the move away from multi-belt drive systems for machinery to the individual wiring of machines for greater economy and flexibility. The list of clients from that period includes C & P Stores, River Mill, Greengate Wood Turning and Wagstaffs Boiler Makers, all situated in what is now Tameside.

This page: *Tameside Leisure Pool.*

Expansion soon meant a much wider geographical spread of work and some of the notable clients during this period were Ever Ready, Associated British Foods, ICL Holborn, Telegraph Newspapers, Vernons Pools, Meccano and Culvers Motors.

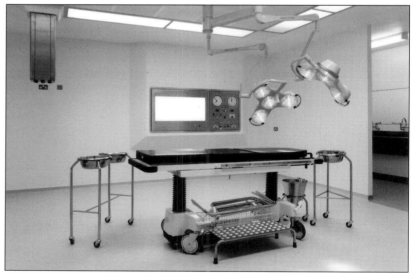

The environment became an important concern in those years. In the early days linked only to the need for cleanliness and safe temperature control, Careys soon developed the expertise of its staff through a variety of work where environmental concerns came into play.

Air conditioning is perhaps the best example of an environmental system which was first developed to protect economic investments in machinery and which was then adapted for the benefit, convenience and improved performance of staff. Enhancing the working environment has been one of the invisible services which companies such as Carey Electrical Engineers have provided to consistently improve the workplace.

Systems for environmental control developed rapidly in the 1960s. Large scale commercial refrigeration is an obvious case and Careys were well placed to carry out work for Frigidaire, Prescold, the Fatstock Marketing Company and the Manchester Dockyard Slaughterhouses. The ongoing attention to bread and butter electrical services meant a continuing link with local authorities; the reorganisation of Local Government in 1974 saw Carey Electrical Engineering registered on those authorities' approved lists of electrical contractors in their own right. This meant that the company did not need to rely on being sub contractor for local authority contracts.

Above: North Manchester Hospital operating theatre.
Top: Carey's managing director and contracts director at the final inspection of Tameside Leisure Pool.

The rewards of inclusion included contracts to rewire substantial public buildings, for example Ashton, Denton and Stalybridge Town Halls.

Combining the expertise in environmental conditions with the links to public service contracts led to work with telemetry systems promoting energy conservation in buildings such as schools, hospitals, offices and prisons.

The sophistication and variety of the company's work has been reflected in innovative training programmes for staff, an area which Kathleen Carrey has focused on since joining the company to work alongside her husband in 1976. Marketing Director and Company Secretary Kathleen soon fostered links with the Chambers of Commerce and their interest in training. In 1988 Kathleen became the first woman to be elected Chairman of the Manchester Chamber of Commerce and Industry within Tameside.

Having a strong interest in training, the company became a pioneer in the training of female apprentices in 1989. Training and a commitment to staff paid off with employee numbers rising from seven in 1990 to twenty two in 1993 and a turnover of a million pounds.

Specialist work has continued with contracts as varied as the first part of the conversion of Styall Mill in Buxton, the first micrarium in the country; work to integrate clean zones, audio systems, intercoms, lights, temperature and humidity for hospitals; electrical work on early-warning stations in Saudi Arabia; clean rooms for Reckitt & Coleman in Bangladesh and Pakistan. The combined experience in these fields left Carey Electrical Engineering well placed to successfully compete for contracts in systems of combined heat and power.

Such combined systems involve the installation of generators into electrical systems. Running times of 16 to 24 hours provide cost benefits from the utilisation of hot water as a by-product. An obvious application for such systems are swimming pools. In 1987 Carey Electrical Engineering won the contract with John Laing Construction to carry out electrical services on Tameside's prestigious new Leisure centre complex. This included power and lighting, public address systems, fire detection, emergency lighting, television aerials, lightning protection and intruder alarms.

Today the company stands on its record of diversity and its tradition of innovation. The progressive staffing increases sustained by an influx of apprenticeships have allowed skills development to balance basic electrical work with specialist approaches. There is a sound base for work with large authorities and a confident application of technical innovations in industry, leisure services and healthcare. Electrical work is complemented by developments in management: from an approach where Albert Carey might once have relied on the back of a cigarette packet to cost out jobs the business now provides a full professional service to clients. The firm has certainly come a very long way since Albert Carrey decided to swap his gas mantles for electric light bulbs!

Below: *Donneybrook/Clarendon Medical Centre.*

Jeans genius

Since the birth of the industrial revolution Manchester has enjoyed an unrivalled reputation as the cradle of some of Britain's foremost companies and of the entrepreneurs who founded them. Whilst many of the largest businesses in the North of England today have their origins in the Victorian era one of Manchester's top ten companies has demonstrated that the city's reputation for innovation, hard work and inspiration are as successful a formula now as they were in the days when Gladstone and Disraeli were conducting their political campaigns. The name of this remarkable company - Joe Bloggs - in itself, curiously, the most unremarkable name imaginable.

The Joe Bloggs group of companies is one of the largest and most successful clothing groups in the United Kingdom supplying all types of outerwear to major retailers throughout Europe. Today however the group has expanded to encompass far more than just its famous jeans. From small beginnings in the 1980s the Manchester company has grown into a financial giant.

In 1964 Nizam Ahmed, an Aeronautical Engineer in the RAF, was transferred from Karachi, Pakistan to England with his wife and their two young children, a son Eathasham, known as 'Shami' and their daughter Bushra. Today Shami and Bushra are internationally known business entrepreneurs famed not only for their wealth but also for Shami's collection of luxury cars and Bushra for her Harley Davidson motor cycle and Porsche 911.

Two years after arriving in Britain, Nizam Ahmed set up a market stall in Burnley, an event which marked the beginning of the Ahmed fashion empire. The market stall was originally nothing but a sideline started up with just £23 of Nizam's wife's money. Nizam used the £23 to buy some nylon stockings to sell. Within five years Nizam Ahmed had opened his first retail outlet, Ahmed Hosiery in Burnley.

Above left: *Shami Ahmed.* ***Below:*** *Shami Ahmed, seen here with Margaret Thatcher.*

In 1980 Ahmed's Pennywise Cash and Carry had been established at premises in Bury New Road, Manchester from where it still operates under the name of the Juice Corporation. While Nizam and Shami developed their plans for wholesale, Shami's mother and sisters ran their retail stores.

Leaving school at sixteen in the late 1970s, Shami, unhappy with the retail business, had pushed his father to explore the wholesale industry: they were a dynamic team.

Shami recalls of his younger days 'I wasn't really interested in the retail business. I wanted to get into wholesale. It was a more specialised business supplying the retail trade. It really started for me in 1976 though when I was working in our wholesale business, it was cash and carry it gave me a great sense of achievement buying and selling everything myself; and I'd do all the deals. Before I left school I used to go to the showroom every day catching the three o'clock bus

each evening. I'd get to work about five o'clock. We would close at six so I was only there for an hour - but did I learn in that hour. The joy in those days was managing the business, me in my shorts and satchel, and the staff working for me, this fifteen year old just doing an hour after school.'

Both Shami and Bushra worked in the family business from childhood. At the age of six Bushra was already helping to pack boxes for her father. 'I was terrible at school' admits Bushra today 'and I was dying to work in the business'. Bushra had begun working for her father packing tights. By fifteen Bushra was the business' main buyer and by sixteen she was negotiating huge buying deals with die-hard businessmen on her own.

In the 1980s Manchester was on an upswing famed as the north's foremost centre for youth, fashion and street culture. With the support and encouragement of their father Shami and Bushra Ahmed capitalised on the upbeat mood and the dynamic dance scene blossoming in their home town to launch The Legendary Joe Bloggs Clothing Company in 1985.

Above centre: Bushra Ahmed with the Harley Davidson. Top: The Pennywise premises.

Shami was just 24 years old when the Bloggs business began, one which would soon make it the first British company to make it into the UK's top ten brand of jeans. Despite intense global competition Shami made the company's name famous and made his first million before he was 25 years old.

How many readers today do not own a pair of denim jeans? In the 1980s the potential market for jeans was even larger. Denim was a major fashion item and yet there was a huge untapped market for quality fashionable jeans at a reasonable price. At the time Joe Bloggs emerged, the marketplace was dominated by expensive imported jeans or cheap low quality ones. Only Joe Bloggs appeared to find the magic combination of balancing cost and quality. Aided by inspired marketing, sales soon exploded.

It was the company's products which captured the spirit of the times. Two years after founding the new company the 25" flare was pioneered by Bloggs as fashion turned back the clock to a look from the 1970s.

Next came the Ventilation Jean with metal rivets down the fly, leg and waistband which became essential summer wear for every fashion conscious lover. Following hard on the heels of the Ventilation

Above right: Joe Bloggs' Ladies B-Free range and the world's most expensive diamond studded jeans.
Top: The Bury New Road premises.

jeans Bloggs' next launched its One-size jeans designed to fit everyone and later also pioneered the return of the drainpipe - in direct reversal of the 25" flare. Joe Bloggs had attained that much sought and seldom achieved miracle of the garment trade: managing to both keep abreast of youthful fashion and simultaneously create new fashions. That miracle was a clear result of two important factors which other firms found it impossible to emulate: Shami and Bushra Ahmed, the leading lights behind Joe Bloggs, provided the firm with that rarest of combinations: youth and experience!

The name of Joe Bloggs was becoming renowned and would soon become even better known as the company announced a sponsorship deal with the boxer Nigel Benn and, never short of ideas to capitalise on the brand name, produced the first Bloggs' toiletries range.

Keeping the name in the public eye was vital: Bloggs produced a range of clothing for Prince and his new Power Generation- Denim inspired by the rock icon Symbol.

And a new 'B-Free' Bloggs range of women's wear was introduced. The firm was moving up market; perhaps nothing symbolised that move more than when Bloggs gained massive publicity when it produced 'the most expensive jeans in the world' studded with the highest quality diamonds worth in excess of $200,000.

If diamond-studded jeans gained a great deal of free publicity other adverts had to be paid for. The 'Everyone Snogs in Joe Bloggs' advertising campaign which ran predominantly in the south of England resulted in 86 per cent brand awareness in Bloggs' target market. Never a firm to miss an opportunity

'Everyone Snogs' and 'Kiss the Bliss' compilation dance albums were released to coincide with the advert launch.

Suddenly, important people were beginning to sit up and take notice of the upstart firm from Manchester: eight years after launching the Joe Bloggs label, Juice Clothing was launched; Princess Anne came to visit the Juice corporation's head office. The following year John Major visited a Joe Bloggs exhibition stand and met Shami Ahmed.

In the business's tenth year a sponsorship deal with cricketer Brian Lara was announced further raising the company's profile and leading directly to the launch of the firm's '375' and 'Five hundred and one runs' clothing range. In the same year, following the same theme, sponsorship of Prince Naseem Hamed and the Manchester Storm Ice Hockey team was announced by Bloggs.

And as if sporting sponsorship were not enough the firm went on to produce its 'Uri Geller Paranormal' range of T-shirts whilst in a different direction the Laundry Registered Clothing Company was launched to sell cheaper clothing.

The following year, the Bloggs' twelfth in business and ready to expand in further directions, Slazenger clothing was launched under a licence now owned by what had become the Bloggs Group.

Above: The Joe Bloggs toiletry range.
Below: Shami Ahmed with Princess Anne.

There was apparently no end to the demand for Bloggs clothing: the 'My First Bloggs' range appeared catering for the new babies of the generation which had first worn Bloggs jeans. And Bloggs went into property buying Wembley Point where the Juice Corporation's London office was established.

Year fourteen saw the birth of the Reflec Clothing plc, a business which Bloggs later joined forces with to produce a range of reflective clothing. This event was followed by the launch of Bloggs' Sports Merchandising with two unique kit sponsorship deals with Bradford Bulls and Preston Northend FC. Not only was Bloggs the sponsor but the company produced a total range of retail merchandise to be sold through the club's official retail outlets.

In the early 1990s Shami Ahmed expanded the family

property portfolio buying retail and office premises across the country, a portfolio worth in excess of forty million pounds by the year 2000. Today the Bloggs empire continues to grow internationally with a 2,000 strong team across England and the world. Despite its size and estimated turnover of up to 80 million pounds a year the Joe Bloggs empire is however still privately owned with the Ahmed family still running the business. Meanwhile the business continues to grow through internal expansion and external acquisitions.

Recently Shami Ahmed formed the Legendary Investments plc, and assigned the running of his part of the Bloggs empire to his younger brother Kashif Ahmed who joined the firm at the age of sixteen in 1992, becoming a company director at eighteen.

Left: Joe Bloggs sponsors Bradford Bulls.
Above (left): Joe Bloggs Drainpipe jeans.
Above (right): Joe Bloggs 25" Flares.
Top: World Cup 1998 Jamaican Football team, nicknamed The Reggae Boyz.

On joining the family firm Kashif had the immediate problem of dealing with the impact of the economic recession on Juice, the company's more expensive and fashionable range of clothing sold mainly through independent retailers. Sales were falling. Kashif's solution was to launch Laundry, a cheaper line of clothing. 'We had to change quickly' Kashif recalls 'retail was in deep recession'. The Juice range was temporally suspended and subsequently relaunched when the recession had passed.

While Shami now develops new areas for growth within 'New Media' and property Kashif manages the Juice Corporation portfolio, which now comprises a variety of labels: Joe Bloggs, Reflec Clothing, Registered Laundry Clothing Company, Jellyfly, Juice and Slazenger. Associated companies, some part of the Pinwise Ltd group, include: Legendary Investments, Hamnett by Katherine Hamnett, Gabicci, Elizabeth Emmanuel London and Major Minors.

Bloggs has branched out into footwear, sunglasses and watches and has even launched a new fragrance called 'Juice' by Bloggs, available at outlets such as Boots and Tesco nationwide. In 2000 Bloggs launched Bloggs Red, an up market range to be sold through select distribution.

The six divisions within the group share a large well stabilised supply base; they utilise selected factories in the UK, Europe and the Far East producing high quality garments at competitive prices. Quality is carefully controlled by Bloggs' own QC staff who visit factories on a regular basis.

Garments are designed in-house, each division

having specialists in both apparel and graphic design; clothing can be supplied on a branded or contract own label basis.

The group employs more than 150 staff who work out of offices and showrooms in Manchester and London.

Distribution is operated on a group basis via a large purpose built warehouse linked by computer to the firm's offices.

The Juice Corporation supplies multiples, store groups, independents and mail order companies across the world from Europe throughout the Middle East and Australasia.

The group's mission statement is 'To design, source, purchase and distribute clothes in such manner as to offer the ordinary person something different at an affordable price'. Joe Bloggs has certainly achieved that objective.

Where will the company go next? For Shami Ahmed, 'the man with the golden touch', it seems that jeans are not enough. In March 2000 a two million pound investment in a new firm, Legendary Investments, saw the value of his investment rise to a staggering fifty million pounds on the day the shares made their debut on the Alternative Investments market. The new company specialises in buying equity in young New Media companies who do their business over the Internet. Internet shares are notoriously high risk but according to Shami Ahmed 'we want to invest in established companies with a good strategy to expand into the net - bricks to clicks. I'm not interested in start-ups'. Perhaps caution is arriving with age, but the world can be sure there is still more to hear from Joe Bloggs and the Ahmed family.

In the meantime does the often Armani-suited Shami Ahmed still wear Joe Bloggs jeans? The answer, readers will be fascinated to know, is, yes he does.

Above left: *Joe Bloggs sponsorship of Nigel Benn.*
Above right: *Brian Lara.* **Left:** *Prince Nazeem.*

Daring to be wise

It is not every school that can claim a history stretching back almost five hundred years. Manchester Grammar School is a member of an exclusive club of educational institutions whose story reaches back to the 16th century.

It was in 1516 that Hugh Oldham the Bishop of Exeter and a Lancastrian by birth, paid five pounds to buy a piece of land near the River Irk in Manchester on which to build a school. By 10 August 1518 when the school opened its doors at Long Millgate the total cost of building had come to 218 pounds 13 shillings and fivepence.

Not content however with simply paying for the cost of building Hugh Oldham also endowed the school with land by the River Irk and with the profits from water driven corn mills. Making the school legally Lord of the Manor, with the power to require tenants to use its mills, ensured future income. The school's first master was William Plessington, who was paid £10 a year in quarterly instalments.

Boys could be admitted to the school from any part of the country provided they suffered no contagious disease such as 'pox, leprosy or pestilence'. And the school rules were strict, reflecting no doubt some of the social concerns of the times: boys were not allowed to carry knives or staves nor to indulge in cock fighting or jousting.

Astonishingly to the present generation of school pupils lessons at the new school started at six in the morning in summer and seven in the winter!

Despite a good start in life the school's fortunes fluctuated over the following two hundred years. Excellent High Masters were interspersed with idle, incompetent or somnolent ones. In the 1750s however the school began to prosper with many new pupils, more than half going on to university.

By 1770 the school found itself now located in a town whose population had doubled in just a few decades to 84,000 and the number of boys had increased from 100 to around 150. An additonal building had been brought into use in 1776 but by 1808 the growth of Manchester had led to an unhappy change in the school's environs. The Long Millgate site had become surrounded by old buildings chiefly occupied by 'poor people in situations neither healthy nor comfortable'. Additionally Long Millgate was the venue for the thrice weekly apple market.

Above: *Long Millgate as pictured in the late 1800s. At the end of the street is the 1880 Grammar School building.* ***Right:*** *Alderley Park Camp in 1904.* ***Below:*** *The gymnasium pictured here in the early 1900s.*

The road was frequently crowded with horses and carts making it difficult for pupils to make their way from the school to the masters' houses where they boarded. Temptation abounded with older boys resorting to the local taverns and consorting with unsuitable women.

Long Millgate stank from the River Irk which had become an open sewer. The boys were expected t o play in the street in front of taverns, warehouses and second rate undertakers. It would however unfortunately take many more years to resolve the school's accommodation problems.

And the question of space would become ever more acute as the 19th century wore on. The appointment of Frederick William Walker, known as 'malleus philosophorum' the hammer of the philosophers, as High Master in 1859 with his stern emphasis on academic attainment led initially to a falling off of pupil numbers.

Word however eventually got around that despite its insalubrious surroundings uncompromising academic excellence could be found at the Manchester Grammar School. By 1873 the school had 500 pupils and by 1876 750.

In 1868 the school had bought more land in Long Millgate for £1,000 and in 1871 took over a new building which had cost £28,000. By October 1880 a gymnasium costing £40,000 had also been added to the school's property . Further building in 1913 transformed dusty narrow Long Millgate into a spacious quadrangle.

It was however too little too late: in September 1931, at a cost of £240,000, the whole school moved to a new site at Fallowfield, a brick, subdued neo-Georgian building. A new and incredibly short school day 9.30am to 3.45pm was instituted to accommodate day boys travelling from far and wide. Today the Fallowfield site bears witness to many more subsequent improvements. Around 210 new pupils from 550 new applicants are admitted to the pupil roll each year. Pupils are drawn from the whole spectrum of social religious and cultural backgrounds, many taking advantage of the numerous and generous means-tested bursaries available to help towards the cost of attending this foremost independent school.

As the school approaches its five hundredth birthday it can look forward to the next five hundred with some confidence that it will live up to its motto, Sapere Aude, continuing to dare its pupils to be wise.

Above: *The Queen's visit in 1965.*
Below: *Morning assembly in the Memorial Hall.*

Gateway to the world

In 1928 when the Manchester City Council was constructing a temporary airfield in Wythenshawe, Chamber of Commerce members commented 'If those interested in aviation can show that arrangements can be made to secure a Manchester aerodrome without undue addition to the city's rates the Chamber will give its approval and sympathy to their suggestions'. Today Manchester Airport is the most profitable municipal airport in Britain. The airport has come a very long way from its humble beginnings: passenger numbers are expected to soon reach 30 million a year.

Britain's first ever scheduled air service began in 1920 from a private airfield in Manchester offering flights to Southport and Blackpool. In 1928 Manchester City Council offered land at Barton near Eccles for the site of a new aerodrome which was to become operational in 1930.

The aerodrome at Barton was to prove of limited use and in 1934 the council approved plans from a new airport at Ringway, the airport's present site. It was a close run thing however with the proposal only being passed by the council 55 votes to 54.

Building work on the Ringway site began in 1935 and the official opening ceremony was conducted on 25 June 1938. In its first 14 months of operation the new airport saw 7,600 passengers. The second world war however changed everything. the last pre war passenger flight taking place on 1 September 1939.

During the war years the airport was used for the final assembly and maintenance of military aircraft along with the training of parachutists: almost half a million

parachute jumps were made over Ringway during this period.

The public would eventually benefit from the three new tarmac runways built during the war. In June 1946 the first post war civilian flight landed at Ringway from Paris and within 7 months 10,000 passengers had passed through the re-opened airport.

The post war period was one of continuous growth. By 1947 the airport's annual passenger throughput had more that tripled to 34,000 and by 1949 extended terminal facilities had to be opened in converted wartime buildings. Two years later the main runway was extended to 1,798 metres.

A boom in air travel led in 1952 to 24 hour airport operation by which time Ringway was handling 163,00 passengers annually. 1952 also saw the first ever transatlantic departure from Manchester airport although only as result of an emergency stopover by a plane bound for Jamaica!

Above: *Air Traffic Control in 1946.* ***Below:*** *An Armstrong Whitworth Argosy freighter in 1962.*

The following year however Manchester introduced a real scheduled transatlantic service to New York. By 1954 the airport had seen its millionth passenger since the end of the war.

Most readers today will be familiar with Manchester airport from holiday package tours; the first package tour to leave from Manchester did so in 1955.

Increasing demand led to the runway being extended to over 2000 metres in 1958 and to the opening in 1962 by the Duke of Edinburgh of a new terminal building costing £2.7 million . By the time the new terminal opened passenger throughput had soared to over a million each year. The 1970s and 1980s were alike decades of continuing growth. In July 1980 the airport dealt with more than half a million passengers in a single month whilst in 1982 a further runway extension took the total length to over 3,000 metres.

In 1986 Manchester airport PLC was formed its shareholders being the 10 metropolitan districts of Greater Manchester: Manchester City Council owning 55 per

cent of the shares with 5 per cent each being allocated to the remaining nine smaller metropolitan districts.

By the end of the 1980s the airport was dealing with over one million passengers a month and handling up to 500 aircraft movements a day. Business was booming and in 1993 Terminal 2 was opened by HRH the Duke of Edinburgh doubling the airport's capacity.

Today there are over 15,000 people working at the airport about 2,000 of whom are employees of Manchester Airport PLC which has the responsibility for the buildings, runways, taxiways and land including car parks. The Company also provides the fire and security services.

The scale of present day activity at Manchester Airport would have been truly inconceivable to Captain A.N. Kingwill who made the first landing at the Wythenshawe site on 2 April 1929 - perhaps almost as inconceivable as it would have been to the inhabitants of the Bronze Age settlement the remains of which were discovered during excavations for the airport's second runway.

Above right: In 1958 the runway was extended to 2,134 metres. ***Above left:*** The construction of the new terminal and control towere was completed in 1962 and was officially opened by HRH The Duke of Edinburgh on 22nd October of the year. ***Top:*** International Pier B in 1974. ***Right:*** Manchester Airport today.

A firm commitment to practising legal affairs in Manchester

Cobbetts is one of the North West's leading legal practices. It is, in fact, the second largest Manchester based legal firm with the largest Property Division of any legal firm in the North West. The firm's history reaches back over the last 200 years and is a story of strong and loyal partnerships and amalgamations that have been gradually developed to build, what is today, a forward-looking concern with a long tradition of high standards.

The first member of the Cobbett family, Richard Baverstock Brown Cobbett practised under the Cobbett name in the 1820s. The firm has seen subsequent Cobbett generations pass through its doors and has borne the family name ever since. Richard Baverstock Brown Cobbett was the son of the famous 18th century politician, William Cobbett. Amongst other things, William Cobbett

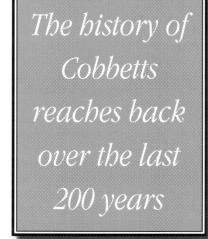

The history of Cobbetts reaches back over the last 200 years

was famed as an Oldham MP, as the author of Rural Rides and for being imprisoned in Newgate prison in 1795 for seditious libel. The practice had a chair which William used in Newgate prison in its offices until 1985 when one of the partners, Henry Stone, kindly took it to the Cobbett Museum in Surrey.

With Richard Baverstock Brown Cobbett, the firm continued to thrive and began building its now traditionally strong links with Manchester's commercial and brewery interests. It was not until the mid 1800s that two new partners were added to the practice. Henry Wheeler, the town clerk of Middleton, joined the firm along with the second generation of Cobbetts, William's grandson and Richard's son, William Cobbett. The firm was re-formed as Cobbett Wheeler and Cobbett and practised under this name until the late 1960s.

Below: Ship Canal House - Cobbetts' offices.

It was in the mid 1800s that Cobbett Wheeler and Cobbett merged with another established Manchester firm, Orford Cunliffe Greg and Co. This firm had been practising in Manchester since 1792 and was originally set up by the solicitor, Mr Duckworth. Mr Duckworth's name can also be traced back to another Manchester legal firm, Davies Wallis Foyster.

The expanded firm continued in its success and in the early 1900s was joined by yet another Cobbett generation. William's son, Walter Cobbett joined the practice and became the third generation of Cobbetts to do so. His father William had been instrumental in the foundation of the Manchester Royal Infirmary and he and Walter both received knighthoods for their good works. There still remains a clock, awarded to William in 1873 for his services to the Infirmary, hanging in the firm's current offices.

Sadly, in 1925 William Cobbett died but, his work and the Cobbett name was carried forward by his son, Walter. Sir Walter was a fastidious and hard working character and every morning, on his way to work, he visited the Waldorf Salon for a shave with a cut-throat razor using only the very best Belgian blades! Sir Walter served the firm until his death in 1954.

During the 1960s another practice, Jackson and Newton merged with Cobbetts, which by then had also incorporated another firm, Wigglesworth and Son into its practice. However, Cobbetts' most important amalgamation did not take place until 1987. It was in this year that another old Manchester firm, Leak Almond and Parkinson merged with Cobbetts to become, Cobbett Leak Almond. Leak Almond and Parkinson had established a large commercial and private practice and was itself an amalgamation of a number of Manchester firms, the oldest of which first started operating in 1834.

The firms came together and began working from Ship Canal House, King Street in Manchester as Cobbett Leak Almond with branch offices at Congleton, Holmes Chapel, Whaley Bridge and Wilmslow. In 1998 Slater Heelis, one of the oldest Manchester firms dating back to the early 1700s, dissolved and Cobbett Leak Almond took two thirds of the firm on.

In 1996 the firm reduced its name to its current title, Cobbetts and continued to flourish. In the year 2000 the firm was awarded accreditation in Investors in People and Lexcel, the Law Society's quality standard.

Today, Cobbetts practises as one of Manchester's largest and oldest firms and offers a comprehensive range of services including company and commercial, commercial property, litigation and private client law. With its long established tradition of providing high quality service and expertise combined with a flexibility and dynamism required to meet the changing needs of today's businesses, Cobbetts is set to continue upholding its reputation of excellence in the North West for at least another 200 years!

Above: Cobbetts' reception.

The spark of genius

It was in 1880 that Joseph Spark founded his joinery business on a site in Higher Road Urmston just 100 yards from the company's present premises. Joseph Spark was originally from Lumphanan near Aberdeen where he worked in the family saw mill. He was enticed to Manchester to work on the city's town hall and enjoyed the Lancashire hospitality so much he never returned to Scotland. Instead the young Joseph Spark settled in Urmston and founded his own building firm.

At the turn of the century Joseph Spark was joined in his business by his son George and expanded the business by starting to build houses and churches. In 1928 four years after Joseph Spark's death in 1924 the firm moved to its existing site on Higher Road and expanded sales of timber and building materials. The firm's saws were run by steam and the sound of the Spark's steam engine became well known in the area.

George Sparks had four sons: Joseph, Norman, Donald and Graham. Joseph junior, the present Directors' father, joined the company in 1927 followed later by Donald. Sadly Norman was killed flying over Belgium during the second world war. Graham entered into a successful electrical career.

During the depression of the 1930s the firm cut back on building work but managed to continue trading and in 1948 became today's limited company.

Joseph Spark's three sons Edward, Robert and Andrew were all destined to join the firm. Robert began as a joiner in 1962 straight from school and, after obtaining further qualifications, moved into the shop and offices. Andrew joined in 1971 after working as a building surveyor. Edward trained as an architect before eventually joining the family business in 1983.

By the early 1970s however markets had changed and the decision was taken to withdraw from construction work and to concentrate on the sale of timber, building materials and joinery.

Above: *Staff outside the sale yard in the 1920s.*
Below: *The premises in 1952.*

New forklifts were purchased and storage expanded with new sheds and land purchased across the road. The sales area increased in stages from under 15 sq metres in the 1950s to the present 300.

Steady expansion continued and in 1987 the opportunity arose to purchase the premises of Moore & Thompson in Lymm. Although a small site this proved a successful venture and with the able assistance of the staff led by Brian Hall the business has flourished. Its situation on a busy main road makes it easy to find and the friendly staff have built a reputation for efficiency.

In 1993 the Old Water Tower in Knutsford came on the market and 'Sparks' took the opportunity to expand once more. The Tower is a unique landmark and provided the firm with a high profile in the town. The depot is run by Andy Betts who was promoted from the Lymm depot.

The firm's depot at Altrincham, previously one of the Builders Mate chain, was acquired 1995. The Altrincham depot fitted well with the firm's geographical coverage of south west Manchester. Today that depot specialises in timber, plywood and joinery products and is being expanded to include most of the group's range of products.

Both the manager Tony Davies, and assistant manager Paul Larty have brought to the company new ideas and expertise which will help develop the group further.

In 1999 Sparks expanded yet again, buying the Middleton depot in Glossop and later that year the busy Altrincham business of John H Holt, a name which has been retained.

The business has traditionally promoted staff from within the firm and those with potential are encouraged to take on responsibility. A typical example is Carl Lever who worked Saturdays part time in the yard at Urmston later progressing to full time before being promoted to sales and who is now the manager of the shop.

In April 1999 James Spark became the fifth generation of his family to join the firm. Jos Spark has come along way since its birth in 1880 but the family hopes it still retains its original policies of sound business skills combined with friendliness, efficiency and most of all good value.

Above: *An aerial view of the premises in the 1970s.*
Below: *Knutsford.*

Going, going...and keeping going

When William Capes decided on a career change in 1826 and gave up his job as a 'Dealer in Manchester Goods' (cotton textiles) to become a chattel auctioneer, he could not have foreseen that the company he founded in the reign of George IV would still be going strong almost 200 years later!

In those early years William Capes had offices at 90 King Street and hired 'The Great Room' in the Exchange as his saleroom as well as conducting auctions on owners' premises.

In 1837 he took into partnership his book-keeper Ebeneezer Smith with their offices now in 14 Princess Street on the corner of Clarence Street; a room was hired over the Guardian Office in Market Street for the auctions.

William Capes died in 1841 and the gavel was taken up by his son Henry William Capes in partnership until Ebeneezer Smith's death in 1851. The burial took place at All Saints Church, Chorlton-on-Medlock. At this point Mr Capes Junior took into partnership his cousin Williamson Dunn who was the brother of Ebeneezer Smith's wife Fanny (nee Frances Dunn).

Disappointed by the turn of events, two of the senior members of the staff, a senior auctioneer and the manager, Mr Artingstall and Mr Hind, their hopes of partnership dashed, left the company and set up in competition a few doors down Princess Street.

Some 140 years later by a curious twist of fate when the proprietor of Artingstall and Hind, Mr Harold Norris, died, Mrs Norris offered the company to

Capes Dunn who bought it - an example of a business turning full circle.

It is interesting to read in Proctor's 'Memorials of Manchester Streets' that after Queen Victoria had made her first visit to Manchester in November 1851, and the Manchester Exchange received its 'Royal' prefix, 'the time had arrived when the 'working-day world' must put aside its Sunday clothes. So Mr Capes, the auctioneer, was forthwith summoned to disperse (in the Town Hall) at the ominous fall of his hammer, all the costly and magnificent paraphernalia - even to the throne and canopy - embellishing the Exchange'.

The company now re-styled as Capes & Dunn, acquired for the first time its own salerooms at No 8 Clarence Street, off Albert Square. The Dunn family owned the Prudential Building which formed the bigger part of one side of Albert Square and the new salerooms were part of this property. The firm prospered and was second only to Sothebys when it came to their regular auctions of important libraries of books.

In 1847 Robert S Pilcher, Auctioneer and Valuer at 78 Mosley Street, gave up his own practice and entered into partnership and took a prominent role in the auction of the 'Highly Valuable Contents' of Bramhall Hall, Nr. Stockport in May 1877.

It is interesting to note that throughout this period and well into the twentieth century the auction catalogues

Top right: An auction catalogue of the Bramhall Hall sale in 1877. *Top left:* Mr Eric Mather. *Above centre:* A caricature of Harry Dunn, Senior.

Eric Mather maintained contact with the firm and when one of the stalwarts of the company and Ray Unsworth's right-hand man, Walter Street, died in 1965 after nearly 50 years continuous service with Capes Dunn, Eric Mather came back into partnership with Ray Unsworth and a young auctioneer called Michael Perry, who had also joined straight from school in 1960.

Further moves took the firm first from 7 Brazennose Street to Whitworth House, 115 Princess Street in 1963 and finally to their present Galleries at 38 Charles Street, off Princess Street, in 1973.

were printed by Charles Severs & Co., on their 'steam-powered press' at Hunts Bank.

The firm continued as Capes Dunn & Pilcher until 1910 when it took its current title of Capes Dunn & Co. and was run by Harry Dunn and Tom Unsworth, both of whom had sons who came into the business. Unfortunately Harry Dunn Junior contracted a germ in the valve of his heart through eating cress and died aged 28. On the death of Harry Dunn Senior in 1933 the family wanted to sell the Clarence Street premises and the company therefore moved into an excellent saleroom at 23 King Street West (illustrated) with Tom Unsworth at the helm with his young son, Raymond Stacy Unsworth, joining the company when he left St Bees' School, Cumbria. At about this time in 1929 Eric Winton Mather also joined Capes Dunn & Co. as an articled clerk, his father paying £250 for the three years training, with Eric receiving £1 per week wages in return.

Unfortunately the premises in King Street West were destroyed by fire in the World War II blitz and during the war the firm had an office only at 27 Brazennose Street; after the war they opened a large saleroom at No 7 Brazennose Street just off Albert Square.

Michael Perry became sole proprietor of Capes Dunn & Co. in 1979 when Eric Mather retired and was joined shortly afterwards by his younger brother Andrew. In the month of August 2000 when Michael Perry celebrated 40 years with the company, Eric Mather celebrated his 90th birthday.

Capes Dunn has been Manchester's premier auction house specialising in the sale of furniture and fine art in three centuries. Today the firm's longevity and its superb reputation combine to make its name as valued by the citizens of Manchester as any of the objects which pass through its auction rooms.

Above left: *Capes Dunn & Co's Auction Galleries at 23 King Street West, 1935, destroyed by fire in World War II.* ***Above right:*** *This rare slipware charger, initialled and dated 1730, was discovered when visiting a client to value a silver tea service. The lady owner, who was going to give it away to the local museum, only produced it as an afterthought. Because it was severely cracked, a cautious estimate of £500-£1000 was placed on it. The plate was subsequently auctioned by Capes Dunn to a telephone bidder for £27,000, prompting the unforgettable Manchester Evening News headline 'Cracked Pot Jackpot in Pottery Lottery'.*

Printed on the memory

For more than a century the family firm of T Liggett & Son Ltd has been a continuing presence in Manchester's printing trade.

The firm was founded in the mid 1890s by two brothers Arthur and Walter Liggett. Their father Thomas Liggett, a Manchester wool merchant, made the money available to start their printing business from a shed in the back garden of Upper Brook Street near Manchester University where the family then lived.

The two brothers Arthur and Walter, both of whom had served seven year apprenticeships in the printing trade, opened their new business on Arthur's 21st birthday in 1896.

Two years later, in 1898 tragedy struck, Walter died of consumption (or TB as we know it today). He was aged just 28. Arthur was left to run the firm alone throughout the Edwardian period and during the terrible years of the first world war. During the 1914-18 war Arthur's business made steady, if unremarkable, progress - a surviving account book of the period showing a turnover in the month of January 1916 of just £37 2s 5d.

In 1925 Walter Liggett, Arthur's eldest son, and named after the boy's deceased uncle, joined the firm. By then the business had premises in Albert Street off Bridge Street on the banks of the River Irwell. No doubt the two Liggetts thought the business might stay there forever, but if so they were sadly mistaken. Fifteen years after the business moved to those Albert Street premises they were destroyed during the Manchester Blitz of December 1940. All the firm's machinery and letterpress type ended up in the river.

Bomb damage and destruction were a fate shared by many firms in that period. Fortunately the Dunkirk spirit prevailed. Refusing to succumb to despair and despite the wartime shortages of paper Walter and the now ageing Arthur picked themselves and their business off the floor. Arrangements had to be made to fulfil existing contracts even if the business had been destroyed. For the remainder of the war years the firm shared the premises and equipment of J & F C Carter on Great Bridgwater Street.

In 1948 two events of great significance occurred: first Arthur Liggett and his son Walter formed the limited company which exists today - and secondly, soon after incorporation, Arthur died.

Above: Thomas Liggett, with his son, Arthur Edmund. Arthur took over the business on his 21st birthday, together with his brother, Walter.

sales to large national organisations. In 1983 Walter Liggett retired and his nephew John became the third generation of his family to manage the firm.

Fresh blood and the challenge of changing times combined to provide the catalyst for more change and growth in the years following Walter Liggett's retirement.

In 1991 the firm's sister company Newton Screenprint was established. Now based in Elsinore Road 300 yards from Liggett's present address, this became the firm's silk screen division enabling 'Liggetts' to offer a complete print service.

Liggetts' latest move came in December 1998 when the firm moved to new premises in Warwick Road South, Old Trafford where it now has over 10,000 sq ft of factory floor and warehouse space. The firm has full mechanical handling facilities and four vans to cope with national deliveries. Clients include many nationally known companies with depots all over the UK from northern Scotland to Cornwall.

The next year, with Walter Liggett at the helm, new premises were acquired in Hulme at 45 Warwick Street in a converted Baptist chapel - complete with immersion bath beneath the floor. Under Walter's leadership the firm's customer base expanded with ever larger clients giving the firm contracts. During the fifties and sixties the firm's major customers included Wilsons Brewery and Cussons Soap.

In 1964 after three years at UMIST John Liggett, Walter's nephew the son of his younger brother Jack, joined the family firm. The business also moved that year to fresh premises in Hewitt Street near Deansgate.

The following years saw a period of gradual but sustained growth - and a great change in printing technology. Those years marked the important transition from letter press to lithographic printing and an ever increasing emphasis on

T Liggett & Son Limited is now a state of the art 21st century printing business. Looking back over the firm's eventful history one can only wonder at the entrepreneurial spirit which has run through the generations taking this family firm all the way from a garden shed to being the major concern it is today.

This page: *The premises today.*

Fred Aldous Ltd - friendly service and family values

Friendly service and old-fashioned values come top of the shopping list at long-established arts and crafts materials suppliers, Fred Aldous Ltd. Family solidarity also scores highly - no less than five generations of the Aldous dynasty have served Manchester folk since Fred Aldous I founded the company back in 1886. Helpful, approachable staff at the Lever Street store and its sister shop in Steeley Lane, Chorley, have an unrivalled knowledge thanks to their constant quest to stay at the cutting edge of craft activities and techniques. Both outlets offer a treasure trove of more than 10,000 products, ranging from acrylic paint and alginate to wax dyes and wooden beads.

The success story started almost 120 years ago, when Fred Aldous I left his native London to launch a business at Elbow Street, near the former Exchange Station. Enterprising Fred imported willow and cane from the Far East to make baskets and hampers for the cotton trade.

By the time his son, Fred Aldous II, took the helm in the 1920s, he realised that the cotton industry was in decline and added a new strand to the business, focusing on arts and crafts. Under the trademark Atlas Handicrafts, their popularity and reputation quickly grew, laying solid foundations for the business that still thrives today.

Fred Aldous II's son Chris, one of seven children, initially pursued a career in farming in Derbyshire, with the staunch support of his father. After selling up in the 1960s, he joined the family firm, becoming managing director in 1972. Now in his 70s, Chris maintains an active interest in the company. Chris's eldest son, Robert, has been involved in Fred Aldous Ltd for 27 years. A graduate with first-class honours in three-dimensional design, he has been managing director since 1992. His sister Susan and brother-in-law Trevor Walker work with him as directors, while his brother Graham, sister-in-law Julie and wife Bernie keep things ticking smoothly at the company's manufacturing base at Peak Dale, Derbyshire. Now Robert's children Mark and Marie and Susan's son Paul are poised to ensure that the company makes a smooth transition into the 21st century and beyond.

Above: Mavis Perkin, who has given the firm over 50 years of service. Below: No 3 Elbow Street - where it all began.

A graduate in art design, Marie is now working alongside her father, while Mark and Paul are both following in Robert's footsteps by doing degrees in three-dimensional design.

Fred Aldous is very much a family firm, and proud of the rich legacy its has inherited. About a third of the workforce were either born or married into the Aldous clan, and the bond shared is extended to include the rest of the employees. Several of the staff have been with Fred Aldous a long time - including the mail order manager, Mavis Perkin, who has worked for the company for almost 50 years. Team work is fundamental to the continuing success of the company.

Customers who call at either of the Fred Aldous stores or reserve goods by mail order can count on an equally enthusiastic reception. One of the company's guarantees is that anyone who contacts it will receive friendly and knowledgeable service - with staff going to any lengths to ensure that they are fully satisfied with the products and information supplied. Many of the team are arts and crafts graduates who specialise in a variety of areas and can offer well-informed guidance and advice.

Above: An exhibition dating from the 1950s.
Right: From left to right (back row): Bernie Aldous, Robert Aldous, Sue Walker, Trevor Walker, Julie Aldous, Graham Aldous. (Front row): Marie Aldous, Chris Aldous, Paul Walker, Mark Aldous.

Neither is Fred Aldous Ltd content to rest on its hard-earned laurels. The company strives to blend the best of both worlds, by combining both traditional and modern. "Although we still sell many items that we have stocked for over a century, we constantly strive to improve and update the variety of goods and services that we supply," says Robert.

Regular workshops are also held, for both adults and children, to encourage people of all ages to satisfy the creative drive that is hidden deep in all of us. The company's quest is, and always been, to share its genuine enthusiasm with its customers. There is nothing quite like creating something that is individual and unique. Fred Aldous provide the raw materials and expertise to turn anybody's bright ideas into reality.

Creating a good impression

Few of us in our lifetimes will have failed to have seen the products of the Manchester Rubber Stamp Company. Whenever one sees the imprint of an office stamp on a sheet of paper the chances are high that the stamp had its origins in Manchester.

The Manchester Rubber Stamp & Flexible Type Company was founded in 1880 by Walter Edward Hughes a chemical merchant whose premises were at 68 Tib Street. The firm originally sold only rubber stamps and ink but later diversified into stencils and general engraving.

In 1920 A Schofield, a stockbroker, took over the company in partnership with H Radford and seven years later in 1927 the business moved to new premises, Tower Works, at 26 Withy Grove.

Like many other Manchester firms the business suffered the problem during the second world war caused by the loss of staff called up for military service and also from difficulties arising from wartime shortages and the restrictions placed on use of materials. Matters were not made any easier when

windows and doors at the Tower Works were blown in during the Manchester blitz - but the firm survived those small 'inconveniences'.

A Schofield died in 1948 and his son J C Schofield then joined the company; H Radford retired in 1953.

The firm remained in the ownership of A Schofield's, son and his widow Alice until 1981 when J C Schofield purchased the balance of the shares to become the sole owner, running the company until his own eventual retirement in 1999.

Geoff A Hewitt, the business' present owner, began his working life with the firm on 8th April 1963. Incidentally, that was also the day that saw Ivy Sinclair begin a long and loyal career as company secretary with the firm. She finally retired in July 1988 after 25 years service. Geoff ran the firm's engraving section from 1970 before becoming a director in 1991.

Above: *The change of address notification from 1971.* ***Below:*** *The firm's premises at Tower Works, Withy Grove.*

The business moved from the Tower Works to its present location at 63 Redbank in 1971, but retained a shop, showroom and distribution depot at 44 Shudehill.

In a grim echo of the blitz 1994 saw a fire in the workshop which set back production for some time. Geoff Hewitt was first on the scene and had to sleep on the fire damaged premises for ten days until they were made secure.

In Queen Victoria's reign the firm began with hand type setting, plaster moulds and gas vulcanisers - today computerised type setting and electric vulcanisers have changed the business beyond recognition.

Throughout the period since Geoff Hewitt became a director there has been a gradual falling off of the rubber stamp business and a tremendous increase in the engraving side of the firm's activity, especially since computer technology has been installed. Engraving now comprises 70 per cent of the business.

Main customers today are blue chip companies, the building trade, electrical trade, engineering trade and local authorities buying a whole range of products such as office signs, industrial labels, memorial boards and plaques as well as the firm's traditional rubber stamps.

According to Geoff Hewitt the firm's main selling points are 'quality, fair prices, the personal relationship we have with customers and the fact that no job too is too large or small.' The firm's mission statement is 'quality, quality, quality' an aspiration likely to be consistently met by the business' technical superiority, a lead maintained by keeping both abreast of the times and ahead of competition with the latest machinery and innovative staff.

Whilst still retaining the old, skilled manual way of engraving, new computerised engraving systems allows the Manchester Rubber Stamp Co or 'MRS' to achieve a more accurate standard of work than the old method. MRS however continues to offer both services.

Geoff Hewitt is proud of his firm's progress and range of products remarking that 'Using computerised engraving equipment and AutoCad drawing packages we can produce everything from company logos to complex mimics using the best quality material such as stainless steel, brass, anodised aluminium, Formica and perspex'.

Under Geoff Hewitt's leadership, helped by his son Alex and daughter Jill, together with works foreman 'Sid' Lawrence Reid, the firm has become a modern thriving business but one which in the future intends to carry on as it always has done - providing quality products and prices.

Traditional virtues do pay; as Geoff Hewitt rightly remarks 'There has always been competition in our industry but most have bitten the dust, whilst after more than 120 years we are stronger than ever!'

Above: *The premises at Red Bank today.*

A cracking good time

How many drivers speeding past the huge chemical works at Urmston give a thought to the fact that the plastic parts of their vehicles may well have had their origins there?

It is now more than fifty years ago that the Carrington chemical site, now home to Montell UK, began production on the 800 acres which were once part of the earl of Stamford's estate. The first sod was cut in October 1946 and full production began in 1951. Four years later the site was purchased from the government by the Shell Chemical Company.

In 1946 at the end of the war the Carrington estate covered an area ranging from marshes adjacent to the Ship Canal across two miles of arable and grazing land to a prisoner of war camp at the site's eastern extremity.

The site original proposed for the massive works had been right on the banks of the Ship Canal but those plans were abandoned due to the instability of the land there and the extra costs which construction would have entailed.

Building on the Carrington/Montell site was much delayed by the appalling winter of 1947 and by the post war shortage of building materials. Older readers may just recall seeing the old aircraft hanger which was brought on to the site and two ex-army huts which were later to see service as a concrete block production factory using sand taken from the estate.

On completion of the development five Catarole furnaces stood out against the skyline sign-posting the finished plant. Catarole was the name given to the cracking of Naphtha, (a component of crude oil) in the catalytic production of Aromatics and Olefins. Production began in 1949 with all units functioning by 1951; they yielded more than seventy different chemical raw materials saving the national economy up to six million dollars a year on the cost of imports. Another contribution, this time to the local economy, was the by-product gas which was piped directly to Manchester's gas works saving Manchester Corporation £250,000 in capital expenditure and 53,000 tons of coal a year.

The production of plastic began experimentally, and on a small scale, in 1955. That same year economic difficulties hit both the business and the country; the government, which had provided much of the initial capital, decided the plant must be sold. The buyer was the Shell Chemical company which paid five million pounds for the business. In fact the boom in demand for plastics which followed hard on the purchase led to many excellent years for Shell which became one of the first to develop polypropylene. New plant and new buildings were introduced and Carrington was linked to the company's Stanlow plant, 23 miles to the west, by four pipelines.

Below: *A 1968 view of the works.*
Bottom: *Part of the workforce in the 1940s.*

The Ethylene 3 cracker was completed in 1967 but as the world economy changed demand fell and by 1982 rationalisation was required. Redundant old plant was cut away and dismantled. The four hundred-foot chimney stack, a local landmark since the 1950s disappeared.

Diversification followed. Opened in 1986 the 23 acre Carrington Business park complex was a wholly owned subsidiary of Shell UK. For many years it had been the base for Carrington Plastic Laboratories and it soon became the home to 140 small businesses employing upwards of a thousand people.
The site became viable again though with a narrower manufacturing base. A new polypropylene plant was built, coming on stream in November 1990. A new polythene plant was built in 1996 the same year as a new plant to manufacture a new polymer product, Carilon.

Montell the current operating company was formed in 1995. Montell is a joint venture company combining the polypropylene businesses of Shell and Montecatini a

world wide polypropylene manufacturer. Although Shell remained the owner of the Batch derivatives and Styrocell plants Montell became the name of the Carrington site and of many others throughout the world.

The year 2000 will see more changes taking place at Carrington, the last of the Shell owned Styrocell plants was sold to a Canadian company called Nova Chemical Corporation, and towards the end of the year Montell will be entering into a new joint venture. The combination of Shell & BASF businesses, namely Montell, Targor and the 50/50, Shell/BASF joint venture business of Elenac will create the largest producer of polypropylene and the fourth largest producer of polyethylene in the world, employing around 10,000 employees.

Montell is a global leader in polyolefins (polypropylene, polyethylene, and catalloy resins) which are produced from propylene, ethylene and butane, the building blocks of the petrochemical industry.

Since the second world war carpets, bottle caps, food containers, packaging, pipes and sheeting and a host of other plastic products have become a familiar part of all our lives and much of that plastic is made by Montell.

As MP Bev Hughes said on the site's fiftieth anniversary 'for as long as I can remember the site has been a vital mainstay of the local economy... the Carrington site has carefully evolved its operations to ensure its future - to a point where it is now totally geared up for its next fifty years'. Given the endless cycle of innovation and change however who knows what the site may look like in another five decades!

Above left: *Some early construction work.*
Top: *A general view of the site in the 70s.*

Royce, Peeling Green - counting the years

With roots going back almost a century the accountancy firm of Royce Peeling Green - RPG - based at offices in Manchester's Hilton Street is one of the best known and highly respected firms of chartered accountants in the city. But how many of the firm's numerous clients know anything of its past?

It was 1911 when Ernest Royce first put up his plate hoping that business would find its way to him. Fortunately it did, and a substantial client base was soon built up in the textile industry.

> *When Ernest Royce began in practice tax relief could still be claimed for the upkeep of a horse*

Ernest Royce was part of a Manchester which is now history. When he began in practice tax relief could still be claimed for the upkeep of a horse!

Royce's clients had to pay income tax at only 9d (4p) in the pound on income above £2,000 per annum and a shilling (5p) on all income above £3,000. Estate Duty had recently risen to an outrageous 15 per cent - but only on estates worth more than a million pounds.

Ernest Royce was a shrewd, intelligent and kindly man - but one of rigid moral principles, something which could upset his clients. It was said that although he inspired respect, confidence and even affection amongst his clients that affection could be mixed with trepidation amongst his more wayward clientele. According to one recollection the occasional defaulter would

Below: From left to right: Stanley Higham, Geoff Norris, Ernest Royce, Geoff Bickerton, Charles Green.

approach the Inland Revenue with unease but had to face his accountant with real fear.

Charles Large was taken on by Ernest Royce as a partner to carry much of the administrative burden; a fortunate choice which would enable Royce to fully enjoy his love of long winter cruises, a passion which endured for so many years that he would live to see his favourite newly-launched cruise liner, eventually crumble to rust and be consigned to the scrapyard.

The current firm however has two roots. In 1935 two young Manchester chartered accountants, Charles Green and Noel Peeling, instituted what was eventually to become the firm of Peeling Green & Co. That firm was founded almost by accident when by chance the two friends had found themselves practising in adjacent premises.

Work poured into their two small practices and through working together the two friends found that they had drifted into partnership. The energy and resilience of youth which was a mainstay of their progress turned to disadvantage however on the outbreak of war in 1939. Both partners and the whole of their staff were very young and for this reason the firm became vulnerable to extinction when many of them were called up for military service. Fortunately the firm employed a Mr G J Primer an accountant exempt from call up and whose mental resolution belied his physical frailty. G J Primer's resilience eventually led him to become a partner in the firm and he, together with Charles Green, kept the firm going through the war years - years which included the destruction of the firm's premises in the air raids of December 1940.

In the immediate aftermath of the war all accountancy firms found an immense backlog of work. It was under

that pressure that Ernest Royce & Co suffered the crippling loss of Charles Large around whom the administration of that firm had revolved.

An amalgamation was proposed, and the partnership of Royce Peeling Green emerged; the older Royce being somewhat shocked to discover that Messrs Peeling and Green had so much confidence in their friendship that they had never had a formal partnership agreement drawn up.

The role occupied by Charles Large was fortunately filled by G M Bickerton an Incorporated Accountant who was then required to study for the examinations of the Institute of Chartered Accountants at night - a challenge he famously rose to by gaining honours in one part and prizes in both.

In 1965 the firm moved to its present premises. Ernest Royce continued to be associated with the firm for sixty-five years living in retirement in Southport until his death at the age of ninety.

The firm remains an independent one, though with world-wide connections. In 1998 the firm amalgamated with the North Wales practice of Phillips Salisbury and now has offices in St Asaph, Denbighshire.

The Practice continues to grow and now has fifteen partners and seventy staff with an annual fee income of £3 million. In addition to the traditional accountancy and audit functions the firm is able to provide expertise in taxation and other financial matters which businesses require in the current era. Further specialisation and expansion has been added by the creation of an Insolvency and Recovery Department and also the Forensic Accounting section. A far cry from the firm's modest origins!

Above: *The firm's Hilton Street Chambers premises.*

This photograph shows the spartan interior of the air raid shelter attached to Sharston Senior School in 1939

Manchester Central Library: Local Studies Unit

Acknowledgments

Manchester Central Library: Local Studies Unit
Chris Makepeace

Thanks are also due to
Peter Thomas who penned the editorial text and
Steve Ainsworth for his copywriting skills